**ADVANCED PLACEMENT
STUDENT COMPANION**
RANDY GABRYS-ALEXSON
University of Wisconsin-Superior
to accompany

Human Geography
Culture, Society, and Space

Seventh Edition

with references to

Human Geography in Action

Michael Kuby
Arizona State University

John Harner
Colorado University at Colorado Springs

Patricia Gober
Arizona State University

JOHN WILEY & SONS, INC.

COVER PHOTO: Jochem D. Wijnands/Getty Images

To order books or for customer service call 1-800-CALL-WILEY (225-5945).

ISBN 0-471-27358-9

Printed in the United States of America.

10 9 8 7 6 5 4 3 2 1

Printed and bound Courier Kendallville, Inc.

TABLE OF CONTENTS

STUDY GUIDE

Introduction

Using the Study Guide

The **Study Guide** is a tool for students preparing to take the Advanced Placement Human Geography examination as a result of using *Human Geography: Culture, Society, and Space* (Seventh Edition). It is organized to provide not only strategies for using the text but also to present a comprehensive introduction to the Advanced Placement Program and information about the end-of course testing program available to students each May.

First and foremost, Advanced Placement Human Geography is a college-level program that goes well beyond the memorization of facts and the simple recall of details. Students are expected to use thinking skills that require comprehension, application, analysis, evaluation, and synthesis. Indeed this is no small order. They must not only master the basic information in the course in Human Geography, but also understand the concepts, trends and relations that give that information meaning. This makes it useful in interpreting the topics that define the Advanced Placement Human Geography course. There are seven such topics that provide the course framework. They are: Human Geography - Its Nature and Perspectives, Population, Cultural Patterns and Processes, Political organization of Space, Agriculture and Rural land Use, Industrialization and Economic Development, and Cities and Urban Land Use.

Because Advanced Placement Human Geography is a college-level course, it is directed at meeting these five goals that complement *Geography for Life: National Geography Standards* (1994) and characterize the objectives of the introductory college course in human geography:

1. to understand and use maps and spatial data sets;
2. to understand and interpret the implications of associations among phenomena in places;
3. to recognize and interpret at different scales the relationships among patterns and processes;
4. to define regions and evaluate the regionalization process;
5. to describe and analyze changing interconnections among places.

Unlike high school textbooks in geography, college texts expect students to assume greater responsibility for their own learning. As a result, college books have fewer study helps and prompts, fewer review questions, and fewer end-of-chapter review sections with attendant exercises such as writing activities and independent study projects. *Human Geography: Culture, Society, and Space* (Seventh Edition) is no exception. It is a straightforward expository development of the complexity of human geography using field notes, case studies, photographs, maps and other graphics to achieve its purpose. In addition, to help students understand the utilitarian aspects of human geography, each chapter concludes with "Applying Geographic Knowledge." This section poses two problem-based challenges requiring students to use what they have learned to develop solutions.

The **Study Guide** has been prepared to help students make the successful transition from a high school course which is almost always teacher-directed to a college course which places the responsibility for learning squarely on the learners. It will assist students in understanding how to master more material in greater depth and with broader implications than has been their experience in most of their high school courses. While Advanced Placement Human Geography as an academic discipline is predicated on theories and concepts about human activities across Earth's surface, its real value is in its utilitarian applications. While *Human Geography: Culture,*

3

Society, and Space (Seventh Edition) is rich with examples illustrating the uses of human geography, the **Study Guide** provides direction for students in the application of its theories and concepts. This is especially helpful when answering the kind of multiple-choice and free-response questions they will encounter on the Advanced Placement Human Geography examination. The pre-test questions provide apt examples of the breadth and variety of questions students can expect on the Advanced Placement Human Geography end-of-course test.

Students should recognize that the **Study Guide** is not a substitute for the text. It will facilitate its use and should be utilized in combination with it. Further, referring to appropriate sections of *Human Geography in Action* (Wiley, 1998) as cited in the **Study Guide** will also help students see the relationship between the "big ideas" developed in the text and their application. This hands-on book contains activities (many computer-based) that encourage students to learn geography by doing geography.

The opening chapters of the **Study Guide** introduce students to the Advanced Placement Program, explain what human geography is, and provide some basic information about the Advanced Placement Human Geography examination with a variety of sample questions. The format for the remaining chapters, which provide a guide to the seven topics in the course outline, is the same. Each begins with a brief essay defining the dimensions of the topic and its place in human geography. This is a context essay and should be read before studying the sections relating to the topic in the textbook. The remaining elements of the chapter are:

- Focus question to direct topic inquiry
- Key word/definitions
- Topic outline/text correlation
- Topic study questions
- Researching the topic
- Connecting to *Human Geography in Action*
- Sample multiple choice questions
- Sample free-response questions

Because each teacher will approach Advanced Placement Human Geography using a different organizational format and a variety of different teaching strategies, students should recognize that the **Study Guide** might not precisely complement their teacher's style. However, the components of *Human Geography: Culture, Society, and Space* (Seventh Edition) will enhance mastery of the content of human geography and prepare students for taking the Advanced Placement examination. The multiple-choice and free-response questions will be especially helpful in providing a model for the examination.

Additional Suggestions for Student Strategies for Course Preparation

1. Keep a set of comprehensive notes on classes in Advanced Placement Human Geography and use them as an integral part of the study regimen.

2. Maintain a personal glossary of terms beyond those suggested in the guide. A significant part of effective preparation for the Advanced Placement examination is vocabulary building.

3. Consider organizing a study group with three or four classmates. The group should meet regularly (at least twice a week and before every test) to compare notes, define key words, raise questions, clarify information, and provide mutual support.

4. Have a detailed and current world atlas at the ready as a reference for locational analysis issues and questions about absolute and relative location, site, and situation.

5. Check the College Board website every several weeks for any updates on Advanced Placement Human Geography and other matters relating to Advanced Placement. The site is: www.collegeboard.org.

6. Maintain a folio of work to serve not only as a record of what has been accomplished (i.e., research papers, special projects, quizzes, tests, etc.), but also as a resource to help review the Advanced Placement Human Geography curriculum in the days immediately prior to the May examination.

Chapter 1

Understanding Advanced Placement and the Testing Methods Used

What is the Advanced Placement (AP) Program?

AP is a program of college level courses and examinations that gives high school students the opportunity to receive advanced placement and/or credit when they enter college. The courses and exams reflect the content and goals of a first-year college course that is offered and widely accepted by a large number of college and university departments in the discipline.

The Advanced Placement Program is administered and managed by the College Board, the same organization that offers the Scholastic Aptitude Test (SAT) and the Preliminary Scholastic Aptitude Test (PSAT) each year.

Each test is developed by a committee composed of college faculty and AP teachers. Members of these Development Committees are appointed by the College Board and serve for overlapping terms of up to four years.

How many students are involved?

Approximately 13,000 high schools throughout the world participate in the AP program; in May 2000, they administered more than 1.3 million AP exams. About 2,900 colleges and universities grant credit, advanced placement, or both to students who have performed satisfactorily on the exams. Some students receive sophomore standing when they have demonstrated competence in three or more of the exams.

How can a student participate in Advanced Placement in preparation for the end-of-course examination?

- through a prescribed Advanced Placement course
- through an intensive regular high school course program (typically at the honors level)
- through a tutorial
- through independent study

The College Board and the Advanced Placement Program encourage teachers, AP Coordinators, and school administrators to make equity and access guiding principles for their AP programs. The College Board is committed to the principle that all students deserve an opportunity to participate in rigorous and academically challenging courses and programs. The Board encourages the elimination of barriers that restrict access to AP courses for students from groups that have been traditional underrepresented in the AP program. For more information about equity and access in principle and practice, contact the National Office in New York. (From www.collegeboard.com)

What courses are presently offered in the AP program?

The Advanced Placement Program consists of 35 college-level courses and exams in 19 disciplines.

Art: Art History, Studio Art , Drawing and 2D and 3D)
Biology
Calculus: AB, BC
Chemistry
Computer Science: A* and AB
Economics: Macroeconomics*, Microeconomics*
English: English Language and Composition, English Literature and Composition, and International English Language (ADEIL tm)
Environmental Science*
French: Language, Literature
Geography: Human
German: Language
Government and Politics: Comparative*, United States*
History: European, United States, World
Latin: Literature, Vergil
Music: Theory
Physics: B, C: Electricity and Magnetism*, C: Mechanics*
Psychology*
Spanish: Language, Literature
Statistics*

* Subjects marked with an asterisk are the equivalent of half-year (or semester) college courses. The others are year-long (or two semesters) college courses.

What is the format of an Advanced Placement exam?

All AP exams contain both multiple-choice and free-response questions. The latter require essay writing, problem solving and the use of a number of critical thinking skills. The multiple-choice section accounts for half of the student's examination grade and the free-response section for the other half.

How are the exams graded?

Multiple-choice questions are machine scored. Free-response questions are scored by about 2,300 college professors and high school Advanced Placement teachers who meet together in teams for one week in June at various college venues in the United States. Team members evaluate individual student answers using a carefully developed set of criteria. Team leaders do frequent cross checks to assure validity and consistency in grading.

Each exam receives a grade on a five-point scale:
5   extremely well qualified
4   well qualified
3   qualified
2   possibly qualified
1   no recommendation

How can a student receive special recognition for performing well on an Advanced Placement exam?

The AP program offers a number of awards to recognize high school students who have demonstrated college-level achievement through AP courses and exams. In addition, the AP International Diploma (APID) certifies the achievement of successful AP candidates who plan to apply to a university outside the United States.

For detailed information on AP Scholar Awards and the APID, including qualification criteria, visit the AP website or contact the College Board's National Office. Additional students' questions may be answered in the *AP Bulletin for Students and Parents*; information about ordering and/or downloading the *Bulletin* can be found at www.college.board.com.

Why has geography been established as an Advanced Placement subject?

Geography addresses a number of important and wide-ranging questions from issues dealing with climate change to ethnic conflict to urban sprawl. A growing number of scholars in other disciplines realize that it is a mistake to treat all places as if they were essentially the same or to undertake research on an environment that does not include an examination of the relationship between human and physical processes in the various regions of the world. Understanding such interactions in an increasing globalized society affirms the importance of geography as yet another tool students can use to inform their world view.

What kind of geography is included in the Advanced Placement program?

It is a college-level course the equivalent of a semester's introductory college course in Human Geography. The course is structured to address human geography's seven core topics: 1) the nature of geography, 2) population, 3) cultural patterns and processes, 4) the political organization of space, 5) agricultural and rural land use, 6) industrial and economic development, and 7) cities and urban land use. *Human Geography; Culture, Society, and Space* (Seventh Edition) addresses each of the seven core topics.

What is Human Geography?

Quite simply, it is the study of people from a spatial and ecological perspective. People are central to geography in that their activities help shape Earth's surface largely through their interaction with the physical environment. Human settlements and structures are part of that tapestry of interaction. It is in that milieu that humans either compete for control of space and resources or work out systems of social, economic and political cooperation.

How is the Advanced Placement Human Geography course organized?

There are seven topics in the program. Each is presented as a separate unit of study. The following is the outline used to develop the Advanced Placement examination. It reflects the structure of the typical introductory human geography course at the college level and is likely to be the outline Advanced Placement teachers will be using with their classes. The **Study Guide** for *Human Geography; Culture, Society, and Space* (Seventh Edition) is also organized to address these topics. The following is the AP summary outline, including the corresponding "Parts" of *Human Geography; Culture, Society, and Space* (Seventh Edition) that address each core topic.

Advanced Placement Human Geography Course Outline

I.   Geography: Its Nature and Perspectives*   (addressed in Part 1 of text)
- Geography as a field of inquiry
- Evolution of key geographical concepts and models associated with notable geographers
- Key concepts underlying the geographical perspective: space, place, and scale
- Key geographical skills
- Sources of geographical ideas and data: the field, census data, etc.

II.   Population°   (addressed in Part 2 of text)
- Geographical analysis of population
- Population distribution and composition
- Population growth and decline over time and space
- Population movement

III.   Cultural Patterns and Processes°   (addressed in Parts 3, 4, and 10 of text)
- Concept of culture
- Cultural differences
- Environmental impact of cultural attitudes and practices
- Cultural landscapes and cultural identity

IV.   Political Organization of Space°   (addressed in Part 5 of text)
- Nature and significance of political boundaries
- Evolution of the contemporary political pattern
- Challenges to inherited political-territorial arrangements

V.   Agricultural and Rural Land Use°   (addressed in Part 6 of text)
- Development and diffusion of agriculture
- Major agricultural production regions
- Rural land use and change
- Impacts of modern agriculture

VI.   Industrial and Economic Development° (addressed in Parts 8, 9, and 11 of text)
- Character of industrialization
- Spatial aspects of the rise of industrial economies
- Contemporary global patterns of industrialization/ resource extraction
- Impacts of industrialization

VII.   Cities and Urban Land Use°   (addressed in Part 7 of text)
- Definition of urbanization
- Origin and evolution of cities
- Functional character of contemporary cities
- Built environment and social space
- Responses to urban growth

* Topic constitutes 6%-8% of the course.
° Topic constitutes 15%-17% of the course.

Is there an Advanced Placement website?

Further information about the AP Program is available at

www.collegeboard.com/ap
or
http://apcentral.collegeboard.com/

Is there an "official" publication explaining Advanced Placement Human Geography?

As with all Advanced Placement programs, the College Board publishes a course description. The one available for Human Geography is the May, 2002 Course Description. Copies are available through the College Board regional offices or online at the above website. A number of other publications are also available to help students and their parents learn more about Advanced Placement and the courses and exams that are available.

Many items can also be ordered on line through the AP Aisle of the College Board Online store at http://cbweb2.collegeboard.org.shopping/.

What to expect with the multiple choice and free-response questions?

The multiple choice questions generally ask you to do one of the following:

1) Recall: These are fact-based questions that require students to recollect specific information
2) Determine Cause: The word because is always a part of the stem in this category of question. The student is expected to identify a reason for something.
3) Interpreting Maps and other Graphics: Students are provided a visual prompt and they must analyze and then identify the correct answer.
4) Except Questions: AP multiple choice questions are never framed using negatives (i.e., which of the following is not an example of cultural assimilation?) Rather, the stem contains "except" as a way of having students discriminate among the possible responses.
5) Effects: This is a modification of the recall type question that the student is challenged to identify why some phenomenon occurs.
6) True/False: From a series of statements or phrases, the student selects the one that is accurate/wrong.
7) Analyzing a Statement: This type of question is a test of reading skills. The student is given a statement several sentences in length and is asked to interpret it.

The free-response questions generally ask you to do one of the following:

1) Analyze: Determine the component parts; examine the nature and relationship.
2) Assess/Evaluate: Judge the value or character of something; evaluate the positive and negative points; give an opinion regarding the value of something.
3) Compare: Examine the purposes of noting similarities and differences.
4) Contrast: examine to show dissimilarities or points of difference.
5) Describe: Give an account of; tell about; provide a word picture.

6) Discuss: Talk over; write about; consider or examine from various points of view; debate; present the various sides of the issue.

7) Explain: Make clear; provide the causes or reasons for something; make known in detail; tell the meaning of.

Advanced Placement Pre-Test in Human Geography

The following are examples of the kinds of multiple-choice and free-response questions on the Advanced Placement examination in Human Geography. The distribution of topics and the level of difficulty are illustrative of the composition of the examination.

Before students begin the course in Advanced Placement Human Geography, they should take this pre-test to assess their level of competence.

Multiple Choice Questions

Directions: Each of the questions or incomplete statements is followed by five suggested answers or completions. Select the one that is best in each case.

1. In the rapidly growing cities of the developing world, the areas where the poorest migrants from rural areas tend to settle are
    A. in slums surrounding the central city.
    B. in squatter settlements on the outskirts of the city.
    C. in the commercial sector.
    D. adjacent to shopping malls and discount outlets.
    E. near places of employment.

2. When people identify the "old neighborhood" as the place where they grew up, which of these kinds of geographic features are they primarily identifying?
    A. geologic
    B. systematic
    C. agrarian
    D. physical
    E. cultural

3. A forward city is a city strategically placed by a national government to identify some aspect of a country's goal for either internal development or for establishing a position of importance in the international community. Which of these cities best represents a forward capital in the modern world?
    A. Beijing
    B. Brasilia
    C. Washington, D.C.
    D. Cairo
    E. Berlin

4. A possible geographic synonym for the Northern Middle East is
    A. Fertile Crescent
    B. North Africa.
    C. Trans-Caucasus.

D. Southwest Asia.

E. East Asia.

5. Which of these was a "pull factor" that encouraged poor European migrants to settle in the United States in the late 19th century?

    A. compulsory military service for males

    B. civil rights

    C. job opportunities in factories and on farms

    D. use of English as a primary language in the public schools

    E. the promise of citizenship for joining the army

6. What has the "Green Revolution" accomplished since it was implemented in the 1960s?

    A. It has brought an understanding that the world's tropical rainforests are endangered.

    B. It has freed the developing countries in Africa from fear of a food shortage.

    C. It has called attention to the effect of acid rain on forests in industrial regions.

    D. It has greatly increased yields of basic food crops in some developing countries.

    E. It has marked the end of such tropical diseases as malaria.

7. Which of the following is the best example of a transition zone?

    A. The Sahel

    B. Great Lakes Region

    C. Nile River

    D. Appalachian Mountains

    E. San Andreas Fault

8. Which of these is an example of sequent occupance?

    A. Mount Everest

    B. South African veld

    C. Indonesian rainforest

    D. Montana cattle ranch

    E. North Atlantic Drift

9. In which of these ways did the principle of intervening opportunity affect migration to Australia in the early days of settlement on that continent?

    A. Information about Australia flowing back to Britain was blocked by the Pacific Ocean.

    B. European cultural influences were slow to reach Australia.

    C. Many British emigrants settled in colonies closer to England rather than travel the great distance to Australia.

    D. People in England perceived Australia to be so hostile an environment that colonization would never be successful there.

    E. The Australian aborigines made settlement difficult in the interior of the country.

10. Austin, Texas has become a center for the manufacture of computers. What major change has most likely resulted in the economy of the city and its region?

    A. The state government has had to relocate because of the increase in the size of the population.

    B. Fewer minimum wage jobs are available now than a few years ago.

    C. Most of the citizens of Austin have been unaffected by this addition to the city's economy.

D. The quality of life has diminished because of the influx of the new workers and their families.

E. There has been a building boom because of the demand for housing for all the new workers and their families.

11. When certain maps identifying the physical features of a place or region include contour lines, their purpose is to show
A. local boundaries.
B. differences in elevation.
C. variations in population densities.
D. latitude and longitude.
E. distances between places.

12. What was the major result of the journeys and voyages of Marco Polo and Christopher Columbus?
A. the development of an international organization to resolve conflicts
B. the discovery of many new medicines and herbal remedies
C. an introduction of representative systems of government to areas beyond Europe
D. decrease in poverty and disease in the world
E. increase in trade among the world's regions

13. Which of these provides the best description of a culture region?
A. an area with similar physical characteristics
B. a section of the world with countries where people of the same race live
C. an area where the people who live there have been environmentally responsible
D. a collection of countries whose people practice the same religion and speak a common language
E. an area historically marked by religious and ethnic conflict

14. "Comparative advantage" is a term in economic geography that refers to a place's ability to produce a product relatively more effectively than another because of its relative location and the resources it possesses. What competitive advantage does Massachusetts have over Illinois?
A. significant untapped offshore petroleum reserves
B. a large annual cranberry crop
C. a small, highly skilled work force
D. an efficient state government structure
E. a world-class system of higher education

15. Which of the following is an example of how early African farmers adapted to the physical conditions in the savanna regions between the Sahara Desert and the equatorial rainforest?
A. The farmers grew the same crops as they had in the coastal regions in North Africa along the Mediterranean Sea, but in smaller quantities.
B. The farmers planted wind breaks and palm trees to protect and shade the crops.
C. The farmers used hoes and rakes instead of plows when planting crops to protect the seeds in the dry soil from erosion.
D. The farmers became nomads because the soil was so poor it could only produce crops for a year of two.
E. The farmers abandoned crop farming and turned to herding cattle.

16. Study the map of Singapore on p. 334 in *Human Geography: Culture, Society, and Space* (Seventh Edition). Its purpose is to demonstrate all of the following except
    A. some of the physical characteristics of the region.
    B. the degree of urbanization on Singapore Island.
    C. the relative location of Singapore.
    D, the island's transportation system.
    E. the economic resources available in Singapore.

17. Which of these capital cities was specifically designed to be a national administrative center?
    A. Ottawa
    B. London
    C. Buenos Aries
    D. Tokyo
    E. Pretoria

18. The international "operational" boundary situation most likely to be the subject of dispute between the two countries sharing it is the one
    A defined by a river.
    B. negotiated by a United Nations commission in 1995.
    C. agreed upon by treaty more than a century ago.
    D. fixed by a meridian of longitude.
    E. determined by a time-honored medieval charter.

19. Maria lives in a city of 80,000 people 300 miles from a metropolitan area with a population of 2 million. Which of the following activities would be the most likely reason for Maria to travel to the metropolitan area in her region?
    A. to purchase a new car
    B. to participate in a sales meeting
    C. to attend a major league baseball game
    D. to arrange a bank loan for starting a new business
    E. to attend a four year college

Note: Consider the content of the paragraph below to answer questions 20-21.

On a daily basis, 250,000 people are added to earth's population. Most are born into nations in the developing world. Tragically, that means that one person in five lives in absolute poverty. One of the results of such deprivation is that almost one billion people in today's world can neither read nor write, and the numbers are growing. As a result, they are forced to live in subsistence economies.

20. Based on the information in the above paragraph, what is a characteristic of the developing world?
    A. low birthrates
    B. stable infant mortality rates
    C. moderate fertility rates
    D. low rates of literacy
    E. stable political conditions

21. This paragraph describes conditions relating to
    A. population distribution.

B. political structures.
C. demographic characteristics.
D. cultural features.
E. relative location.

22. Which of the following contains the essential components for a well-integrated state?
A. It has a well-developed primary core area and a mature capital city.
B. It has a federal system of government and enjoys good relations with its neighbors.
C. It has a reliable and well-developed infrastructure and an economy that is service-based.
D. It has a unitary model of national organization and relies upon a strong military force to support the government's policies.
E. It has its total territory divided into many governmental units and an administrative system set up to implement the policies of the central government.

Note: Examine this chart to answer question 23.

Major Exports of Selected Countries

Country A	Country B	Country C
oil	cars	computers
natural gas	televisions	airplanes
coconuts	cameras	wheat

23. Which country most accurately represents the export pattern in Column C?
A. United States
B. Sweden
C. Singapore
D. Japan
E. Australia

24. Which of these descriptors best identifies the concept of culture as applied by human geographers?
A. a civilized pattern of behavior
B. an expression of artistic qualities found in music, drama, and dance
C. a combination of habits relating to such qualities as personal hygiene and eating habits
D. learned patterns of behavior common to a group of people
E. habits of mind learned through formal schooling

25. One of the reasons for Japan's great industrial achievement is that as the country began to modernize, the Japanese followed a policy that
A. opened their country to European immigration.
B. exploited the rich resource base their country possesses.
C. imitated many of the industrial techniques of developed nations.
D. embarked upon a policy of colonization in the sparsely settled islands of the Pacific.
E. encouraged proselytizing by Christian missionaries.

Free-Response Questions

Directions: As a practice exercise, students should develop answers to these two free-response questions. Both are presented as case studies and require problem solving. Responses should reflect a clear understanding of what each question expects of the student. The Roman numerals in **bold** type accompanying each question identify the topic on the course outline that the question addresses.

1. A highly successful development company is planning to purchase a strip of land along the coast of North Carolina to build a resort community for vacationers and retirees. One of the most attractive features of the site is a fairly well preserved tidal marsh. The company's engineers have conducted several feasibility studies over the last year to determine how to use the property in a profitable yet responsible way. Of the human activities listed here, select the one that is likely to have the least negative impact on the ecosystem of the tidal marsh. Explain the rationale for your choice

   A. draining a part of the marsh to build a marina for pleasure boats
   B. constructing a pontoon bridge across the marsh with several landfill parking   lots and access roads along the way for summer tourists who will visit the marsh using skimmer boats operated by the development company
   C. planning to make the marsh into a fish and game preserve for seasonal hunters
     and year-round fishermen
   D. donating several thousand acres of the marsh to the National Park Service to become a part of its national seashore conservation project and developing the rest as a high-rise condominium community for retirees **Topics I, II, and IV**

2. You live in a Maine resort town in an inlet on the ocean. A few years ago, the town council contracted to build an aquarium and develop a marina in the harbor for pleasure boats. It has been very successful attracting far more tourists than predicted. The local merchants and the marina operators welcome the new additions because both have created jobs and profits. However, other local people whose livelihood is fishing, complain that they cannot meet their catch quotas because the harbor waters where they previously dug for clams, oysters, and other mussels has shrunk. It is also dangerously polluted from over use.

As an environmentalist and a cultural geographer sensitive to the special character of coastal New England towns, you have been hired to study the situation and recommend a solution to the problem. After several months of research involving hundreds of hours of field study, you prepare to write your report. It begins with this sentence: "While the resources in this community are limited, a compromise between those promoting tourism and those anxious to protect the local fishing industry is possible."

Discuss the solution you propose to resolve this conflict about human needs and wants among the two competing groups in the town   **Topics III and V**

•••••••••

Answers to Multiple Choice Questions: Each answer is followed by the primary topic title from the outline of the Advanced Placement Human Geography program plus citations from *Human Geography: Culture, Society, and Space* (Seventh Edition). Students can refer to these pages for information explaining and clarifying the correct item choice. Refer to R-page citations in the reference sections of the text.

1. B Topic VII   Urbanization. (76-78, 81-85)
2. E Topic VII   Urbanization. (24-25, 339-340)
3. B Topic VI   Industrialization and Economic Development. (227)
4. D Topic VI   Industrialization and Economic Development. (40-map)
5. C Topic II   Population. (81, 83-84)
6. D Topic V   Agriculture and Rural Land Use. (307-308)
7. A Topic I   Geography: Its Nature and Perspectives. (44-47)
8. D Topic III   Cultural Systems and Change. (25)
9. C Topic III   Cultural Systems and Change. (85)
10. E Topic VI   Industrialization and Economic Development. (396-403)
11. B Topic I   Geography: Its Nature and Perspectives. (R section)
12. E Topic III   Cultural Systems and Change. (24-25)
13. D Topic III   Cultural Systems and Change. (7)
14. B Topic VI   Industrialization and Economic Development. (372-373)
15. C Topic V   Agriculture and Rural Land Use. (280-281)
16. E Topic VII   Urbanization. (234)
17. A Topic IV   The Political Organization of Space. (335, 343)
18. B Topic IV   The Political Organization of Space. (215-218)
19. C Topic VII   Urbanization. (335-336)
20. D Topic II   Population. (76-78)
21. C Topic II   Population. (76-78, R section)
22. A Topic IV   The Political Organization of Space. (226-227)
23. A Topic VI   Industrial and Economic Development. (400-401)
24. D Topic I   Geography: Its Nature and Perspectives. (5,16)
25. C Topic VI   Industrial and Economic Development. (369-374)

Answers to Free-Response Questions. In answering these two questions, it is important to respond to the operative verb. In the first question, it is "explain" and in the second, it is "discuss."

1. In this question, students must first identify the option they select and then make clear the reasons for their choice. This involves presenting and developing them in detail. The three key elements that must be addressed are the nature of ecosystems and the need for environmental responsibility, the economic dimensions of the choice students make, and how human decisions and the use of the environment interact. The response will be most meaningful and persuasive when put in the context of cultural ecology (Part 1). For background information in the text, use Part 8 on "The Geography of Modern Economic Change" and R sections in the glossary.

Key words that should be included in the answer:

cultural ecology	development	ecosystem
environment	human/environmental	interaction
human geography	models	region

2. In this question, student responses should examine the two positions and present both sides of the issue in a fair and objective manner. Such a presentation serves as background to the solution students must propose. That solution must be stated succinctly and forthrightly. The most likely solution is one promoting planned development and a local regulatory commission. Chapter 6 in *Human Geography in Action* will serve as a helpful resource in providing some models for dealing with the issues of employment, specialization and economic development. Because the impact of tourism is a key factor in addressing this problem, students will want to refer to Part 9 of the text.

Key words that should be included in the answer:

comparative advantage	tourism	planned development
regulation	ecology	location
spatial perspective		

Chapter 2

Defining Geography: What Is It? What Does It Mean?

Note to the student: When you finish reading this essay and Part One of the text, you should be able to do two things:
- describe geography in a single paragraph;
- explain the importance of geography in a three paragraph essay using strong topic sentences to introduce each paragraph and incorporating the key words listed below in the body of the essay.

Key Words:
geography	spatial	human/physical systems
location	place	interaction
themes	traditions	environment
space	scale	patterns

Geography as a discipline is confounding. Trying to define it is elusive because it is so imprecise. To understand geography is not necessarily to know what it is. Instead it is to understand what it encompasses. Human Geography stresses the importance of spatial organization and the location of people, places, and events, and the connections among places and landscapes – in the understanding of human life on earth. As a result, geography is more meaningful when it is described rather than when it is defined.

Many people perceive geography as simply an exercise in place location. That means being able to answer a single question about a place: Where is it? If, for example, Chicago is identified as a city in northeastern Illinois on the southwestern shore of Lake Michigan, that information has indeed answered the "Where is it?" question. To be even more accurate, data on the city's latitudinal and longitudinal coordinates could be given showing it at 41°49'N, 87°37'W.

Even though such identifiers about Chicago's location are accurate, they bring the inquirer only to the threshold of really getting the total "geographic" picture because there are other more important and more interesting questions to pose and answer about places. Chicago becomes far more meaningful when it is understood in the context of the answers to these questions:

- Why is it where it is?
- How did it get there?
- What does it look like?
- Where is it in relation to other places?
- Why is it important?
- How is it connected to other places in its region, its country, its continent, and the world?
- How does it interact with other places?

Learning the answers to these questions begins to give Chicago dimension and meaning since they identify both its physical (natural) and human (cultural) features. They also provide a context for studying the spatial characteristics of the city by making clear both its site (i.e., its physical setting) and its situation (i.e., its location in relation to other places). More importantly, the interaction between Chicago's physical and cultural features help explain its role as an immensely diverse urban magnet that for almost two centuries has drawn people from across the world to live and work in its neighborhoods and the hinterland beyond. Photographs and maps showing the tracks that lace the city's rail yards like so many scrimshaw etchings and the mile-long runways accommodating thousands of flights daily at O'Hare International Airport reveal a tapestry of transportation networks moving people, goods, ideas, and services to and from all corners of Earth. And the communications aerials atop Sears Tower and the Hancock Building in the central business district (CBD) send images and words that inform, entertain, and challenge people around the globe. As a manufacturing core and marketplace for making most of the world's candy and wholesaling everything from elegant silks to finished steel for bridges and buildings, Chicago provides a commercial function that helps make the economy of the United States the world's largest and strongest.

Certainly a list inventorying the city's role that derives from its location could go on and on, but the point is clear. Wherever a place is only marks the beginning of giving it definition and establishing its importance among other places. By examining the spatial aspects of a place's location and how the people living there function and make their livings confirm that geography is not so much about the memorization of facts but about asking questions, solving problems, and making nformed decisions about the physical and human complexities of the planet.

More than anything else, geography is an integrative discipline. That is why it is so difficult to define. It brings together the physical and human systems of the world in the study of people, places, and environments.

Human Geography: Culture, Society, and Space (Seventh Edition) provides some valuable insights about the meaning, traditions, and themes of geography. The chapter's introductory sentence serves as an appropriate point of departure for the study of the Advanced Placement program in Human Geography. "Geography is destiny," the authors assert, and proceed through the book's development to describe how exactly this is so. In the course of study, geography is portrayed as making its subject matter Earth's surface and the systems that shape it, the relationships existing between people and their environments, and the connections between people and the place where they live, work, play, and visit. It becomes the process of knowing and understanding spatial interaction. Ultimately, as a special habit of mind, geography is a way of thinking about the world and its people through the prism of place and space.

At the beginning of this chapter the student was told that upon completion of reading this essay and Part One of the text, they should be able to do two things:
  • describe geography in a single paragraph;
  • explain the importance of geography in a three paragraph essay using strong topic sentences to introduce each paragraph and incorporating the key words listed below in the body of the essay.

Key Words:	geography	spatial	human/physical systems
	location	place	interaction
	themes	traditions	environment
	space	scale	patterns

As additional practice for the Advanced Placement examination, complete the two bulleted assignments above before proceeding. Put these two brief essays away until you finish the course to see how this course of study may change your perception of geography and what it encompasses.

Chapter 3

Advanced Placement Topic I

Geography: Its Nature and Perspectives

Note: Questions on this topic will comprise five to ten percent of the Advanced Placement examination. Material relating most closely to this Advanced Placement topic can be found in Part One of the text.

A. The Topic in Context - An Introduction

As the study of Earth as the home of the human family, geography examines places from a spatial and ecological perspective. To do that, it is necessary to use a variety of tools because the discipline is so complex. It bridges many areas of inquiry and in the process, reveals the relationships that exist between and among them. Napoleon's ill-fated invasion of Russia in 1812, for example, was as much a geographic event as it was an historic one - perhaps even more so. Distance, weather, and over-extended supply lines were as much his enemy as the punishing pursuit of the Russian army after the French general was forced to leave Moscow in the dead of winter. Hunger, disease, and the bitter cold forced Napoleon to abandon the campaign. His retreat across the seemingly trackless Northern European Plain was far more devastating than the enemy's guns. When he returned to Paris in the spring, his army of half a million soldiers had dwindled to a rag-tag lot of fewer than 30,000.

What Napoleon needed was a persuasive geographer with detailed maps, weather data, and an understanding of the distances separating Paris from Moscow. By dismissing scale, the vastness of the European Plain, its weather patterns, the obstacles of the region's physical features, and all other spatial associations, Napoleon ignored the processes of the physical world and allowed ambition to blind him to the geographic realities he and his army faced. More than any other factor, it was geography that shaped his destiny. Ultimately, it made his final defeat at Waterloo in June, 1815 inevitable.

If Napoleon had lived at the end of the nineteenth century rather than at its beginning, he would have had the benefit of three geographic theoreticians (Friedrich Ratzel, Sir Halford Mackinder, and Nicholas Spykman) who hypothesized about the relationship between location of a nation in Eurasia and political dominance. The speculations of these scholars typify the work of human geographers in suggesting general principles governing locational behavior and processes. When geographers embark upon such speculation, they often create models to replicate and explain reality. Even though such models are idealized representations of human phenomena, nonetheless they offer a means of focusing on issues affecting events and decisions in the real world. If Napoleon, then, had a geopolitical model to inform his judgment, perhaps he would have sought conquests along the Black Sea rather than along the Baltic.

Geography, as an academic discipline, is rather young. Two major periods are defined that help illustrate the emergence and evolution of geographic thought. The Classical Period extends for thousands of years until 1859 during which very little attention was given to the definition of separate fields of study. Because knowledge of the world was limited a scholar could become master of all. So prior to 1859, a Greek philosopher was as much a scholar of history as of geography. Alexander von Humboldt is often thought of as the last person to claim universal scholarship. The Modern Period began in the latter part of the nineteenth century. It is defined by the emergence of the professional field of geography.

The purpose of this topic in the Advanced Placement course is to encourage students to think geographically: to recognize that to make sense of Earth's complexity, geographers organize the world into spatial regions; to understand that geography has a special vocabulary which finds graphic representation on maps, in data bases, in photographs, pictures and other illustrations, and through field observation; and finally, to begin to use the habits of mind that distinguish geography from other systems of inquiry to define and interpret the world. The topic outline is an introduction to human geography and identifies what lies ahead in the course of study.

B. Focus Question to Direct Topic I Inquiry

When students have concluded their study of this topic, they should be able to prepare a comprehensive answer to this question:

Explain how a human geographer interprets the spatial and ecological perspectives of Earth using maps and other geographic representations, tools, and technologies in order to acquire, process and report information about peoples and their cultures.

C. Key Words/Definitions

Students should be able to define these terms and use each in such a way that its meaning is clear in the context of a sentence. Example:

Definition - <u>Mental map</u>: an image an individual has of an area as determined by perception, impression and knowledge; also known as a cognitive map.

Context sentence - As people become more familiar with places through study or field visits, their <u>mental maps</u> become increasing more accurate and precise.

Note: The citations within the parentheses next to each term identify the page numbers where it is defined and/or discussed in *Human Geography: Culture, Society, and Space*. Many terms are also included in the Glossary.

distribution (5)
field study (2, model on introductory page of each chapter)
map (9,16)
mental map (17)
model (Reference section)
pattern (5)
perception (17, 29-30)
perspective (ecological, spatial) (5-6)
place (8)
region (formal, functional, perceptual) (16-17)
scale (9-10)
site (Reference section)
situation (Reference section)

system (22)
themes (6-7)
toponymy (147-148)
traditions (5-6)

D. Detailed Topic Outline/Text Correlation

Note: The citations within the parentheses identify the page numbers where information within the outline can be located in *Human Geography: Culture, Society, and Space* (Seventh Edition).

I. Topic - Geography: Its Nature and Perspective

A. Geography as a field of inquiry (p. 4-8, 23 with special attention to geography's five organizing themes and four traditions)

B. Evolution of key geographic concepts and models associated with notable geographers (Note: Students should be able to identify the following geographers, briefly explain the theory each developed, and indicate why the theory/model is important for human geographers. Preparing a chart using the references cited here will serve as a "handy go-to" document when specific geographers and their theoretical models are noted in class lectures and discussions as well as in other topics in the course of study.)
John Borchert, 335; Lester Brown, 537-538; Ernest Burgess, 336-337; Judith Carney, 309; Manuel Castells, 422; Walter Christaller, 344-346; Aharon Dogopolsky, 130; Clifford Geetz, 21; Peter Hall, 422; Chauncey Harris, 337, 342; Richard Hartshorne, 214; David Harvey, 424; M. J. Herskovits, 21; E. Adamson Hoebel, 21; Homer Hoyt, 337; Ellsworth Huntington, 32; Mark Jefferson, 324; William Jones, 125; August Lösch, 371, 376; Thomas Malthus, 69; T. G. McGee, 360; Richard O'Brien, 425; Friedrich Ratzel, 224; Carl Sauer, 24, 28, 38, 277; Ruth Leger Sivard, 495, 503, 507; Gideon Sjoberg, 324; John Snow, 412; Nicholas Spykman, 225; Johann Heinrich von Thünen, 283; Immanuel Wallerstein, 399; Alfred Weber, 371; Alfred Wegener, 5, 515.

C. Key concepts underlying the geographic perspective: *space, place, scale, change, perception, region, spatial association, pattern, process, relationship* (Note: Part One provides an excellent introduction to the concepts and perspectives identified in this section. The glossary provides definitions for most of these terms as well. Students should also look up the meaning of "systems" since it is an integral concept to understanding both human and physical geography.)

D. Key geographical skills
    1. How to use and think about maps and spatial data sets (9-11)
    2. How to understand and interpret the implications of associations among phenomena in places (9-11, and Toponymy, 147-148)
    3. How to recognize and interpret at different scales the relationships among patterns and processes (4, 9)
    4. How to define regions and evaluate the regionalization process (7, 16-17, 29-32)
    5. How to characterize and analyze changing interconnections among places (Language and Trade, 138-141, Patterns on the Map, 400-401)

E. Identifying sources of geographic ideas and data: field study, observation, and analysis (Note: The authors of the text have provided several helpful features illustrating the practical applications for using geographic sources, acquiring geographic data, and doing field study using observation and analysis. Students should pay special attention to these features that are common to every chapter: *At Issue, From the Field Notes, Focus On, and Applying Geographic Knowledge*).

E. Topic I Study Questions - Geography: Its Nature and Perspectives

Note: These questions will help guide the student's study of Topic I as well as serve as a review to assure knowledge and understanding of its content.

1. What are basic concepts human geographers use to study people and their cultures?
2. What is a system? Distinguish between a human and a physical system.
3. Explain why maps are considered "the language of geography." List some of the many ways they are used.
4. What is a mental or a cognitive map? Why are they important? How are they developed and improved?
5. Why are theoretical models important to human geographers? How do they relate to real-life situations?
6. Define a region. What types of regions are there? Give an example of each.
7. Explain these two analogs.
> A. Place is to geography what time is to history.
> B. A region is to a geographer what a personality type is to a psychiatrist or an era to an historian.
8. Why are maps, charts, tables, pictures and other graphics so important in the study of geography?
9. How are field studies used as tools for geographic inquiry and investigation?
10. What is toponymy? Explain why understanding toponymy reveals a great deal about what people do and value in a particular place and location.

F. Researching Topic 1 - Geography: Its Nature and Perspectives

Students will find that preparing short research papers (i.e., up to five pages) as part of the study of a topic is an effective means of deepening their understanding of its meaning and purpose within the realm of human geography. Such research serves not only as an introduction to the resources available about the topic but also as a strategy for applying the skills of organization and presentation essential to responding to the extended answer questions on the Advanced Placement examination in Human Geography.

The topics listed below serve as suggestions for the kind of research and investigation students can undertake. Each research paper should be written from an outline developed from the student's research with a brief introduction stating the hypothesis (i.e., a tentative explanation of facts tested by the investigation in the paper). A hypothesis, then, is merely a theory or a speculation that the researcher sets out to prove or disprove.

If, for example, a student wants to inquire into some aspect of toponymy (D. 2 in the Topic I outline), an appropriate hypothesis might be: Local place names are an important part of any cultural landscape. In the introduction, the hypothesis will be examined in the frame of reference of toponymy: what it is, and why and how it is important to human geographers. Including some specific illustrations (e.g., historical or religious examples such as Constantinople having a name change to Istanbul, or what place names like Corpus Christi and Santa Cruz infer about the beliefs of the of the first settlers) will add interest value as well as clarify the purpose of the hypothesis.

The body of the research paper provides the detail addressing the hypothesis. It provides precise information derived from the research the student has done and also follows the outline that has been prepared. As a result, the arguments should be well organized and logically presented. Including anecdotes and examples will make the paper more convincing and also more persuasive.

The final part of the research paper is the conclusion. That is the section providing a summary of what the student has argued and joins those arguments to the hypothesis. The purpose of the conclusion is to demonstrate why the hypothesis works (or does not work). It is the part of the paper where the writer rests the case.

To be convincing, research papers should contain citations and bibliographies. That gives them credibility. Such references also help validate the arguments the student presents. Because there is no *one* correct way to document research these days, teachers will provide the necessary guidance and direction for students relative to format. There are several widely used style manuals available. However, the three most often used to guide reporting research in human geography include:

American Psychological Association. *Publication Manual of the American Psychological Association*. 4th ed. Washington, D. C.: American Psychological Association. 1994.

Gibaldi, Joseph *MLA Handbook for Writers of Research Papers*. 4th ed. New York: Modern Language Association. 1995.

The Chicago Manual of Style. 14th ed. Chicago: University of Chicago Press. 1993.

Some Suggested Research Topics for Geography: Its Nature and Perspectives

Maps as the Language of Geography
Using Theoretical Models in Human Geography
Who Invented Geography?
Geography's Four Traditions: A Study in Perspective
Why Regionalize the World?
The Value of Field Observation in Geography
The Use of Geographic Data Bases in the Information Age
Defining Human Geography
How One Geographer Made a Difference (A case study on one of the geographers cited in part B of the outline for Topic I)
Applying the Spatial Perspective in Human Geography

G. Connecting to *Human Geography in Action*

Chapter 1 (1-1 to 1-23 plus the CD) serves as a solid introduction to human geography and reinforces many of the inclusions in the outline for Topic 1. The chapter is especially helpful in presenting different types of maps and showing students their uses and value. The CD encourages students to manipulate data on thematic maps, interpret new configurations, and draw fresh inferences. The exercises are practical and show the applications of geography to real world situations.

H. Sample Multiple-Choice Questions

These questions are typical of the kinds of questions students can expect on the examination in Advanced Placement Human Geography. Reviewing the pre-test section on multiple-choice questions in Chapter 1 of the **Study Guide** will help students better orient themselves for selecting the appropriate answer in the sample questions included here.

Directions: Each of the questions or incomplete statements is followed by five suggested answers or completions. Select the one that is best in each case.

1. The members of the city council of a mid-sized United States city have recently contracted with a team of geographers specializing in locational analysis to do a site study for a proposed regional airport. The council wants some recommendations about a site that they have selected for a new airport. One of the problems the team might have in examining a series of aerial photos of the proposed site is
    A. there is too little detail showing land use activities.
    B. scale is difficult to determine.
    C. the details of relief are missing.
    D. the distribution of vegetation is obscure and imprecise.
    E. the volume of detail disguises the purpose of the map.

2. Transplanting rice as a labor intensive activity done by hand in Sichuan Province in the People's Republic of China best represents the
    A. theme of absolute location.
    B. the application of Pattison's culture-environmental tradition.
    C. similarities among the world's agricultural regions.
    D. method of rice production used universally.
    E. relationship between humans and their physical environment.

3. Which of geography's five organizing themes examines the arrangement of road networks?
    A. location
    B. place
    C. human/environmental interaction
    D. movement
    E. region

4. A researcher for a non-governmental relief agency is developing a data base on the human geography of equatorial Africa. What is an example of a correct column label that he should include on the chart?
    A. Gross Domestic Product Per Capita
    B. Key Categories of Vegetation
    C. Annual Precipitation Totals
    D. Major Landforms
    E. Acreage of National Parks/Game Preserves

5. Which one of these terms does a geographer use to identify such human phenomena as roads, ports, and rail systems?
    A. infrastructure
    B. functional specialization
    C. centripetal forces

D. mercantilism

E. theoretical models

6. Which of these descriptors best identifies the concept of culture as applied by human geographers?

    A. a civilized pattern of behavior

    B. an expression of artistic qualities found in music, drama, and dance

    C. a combination of habits relating to such qualities as personal hygiene and eating habits

    D. learned patterns of behavior common to a group of people

    E. the oral tradition on which a society's customs are based

7. What does a large-scale map show?

    A. a large area

    B. an unbalanced area

    C. a small area

    D. an undefined area

    E. an uninhabited area

8. When geographers examine a map to determine the way places and other phenomena are presented on the cultural landscape, they are using a

    A. pattern analysis.

    B. spatial perspective.

    C. distribution measurement.

    D. scale measurement.

    E. diffusion model.

9. The map on 16 (Figure 1-6) in the text is an example of a

    A. thematic map.

    B. equal frequency map.

    C. an isoline map.

    D. a comparative analysis map.

    E. choropleth map.

10. Which of these is an example of a perceptual region?

    A. Northeast Corridor

    B. Corn Belt

    C. Central Division of the National Football League

    D. Metropolitan Tokyo

    E. Dixie

Answers: 1) C 2) E 3) D 4) A 5) A 6) D 7) C 8) B 9) A 10) E

I. Sample Free-Response Questions

These questions are similar to the free-response items likely to be on the Advanced Placement Human Geography examination.

1. Explain why theoretical models are helpful tools for human geographers in the studies they make of cultural phenomena. Provide two examples as illustrations.

2. Define spatial and cultural perspectives and compare the two to show how they are essential to the work of human geographers.

3. Explain why geographers divide the world into regions. Include illustrations describing at least two types of regions.

4. Discuss the importance of geography as a visual discipline where maps and other graphics are used to interpret the complexity of Earth.

5. The authors of the text observe in the introductory chapter: " People's perceptions of places and regions are influenced by their individual mental maps as well as by printed maps." Evaluate this statement in terms of what it suggests about the influence of culture and the importance of place.

Chapter 4

Advanced Placement Topic II

Population

Note: Questions on this topic will comprise thirteen to seventeen percent of the Advanced Placement examination. The majority of information needed to prepare for this section of the test can be found in Part Two of the book.

A. The Topic in Context - An Introduction

Population geographers study the distribution of people across Earth's surface. It is in those distributions that they are able to discern patterns of growth and decline as well as learn why some groups live longer and healthier lives than other groups. In the broadest sense, these geographers are interested in demography, which is an investigation of all the factors that influence the characteristics of individual populations. Why, for example, is herding so much a part of the culture of the arid and treeless African Sahel? Why is the small but tidy nation of the Netherlands one of the most densely peopled places on the planet but at the same time, one of the most economically successful? Why is it that tiny Haiti with its teeming numbers cannot replicate the Dutch experience? Why can Indonesia support a population numbering in the scores of millions on an elongated archipelago that sprawls across the Pacific Ocean while Nunavut, Canada's newest territory the size of Mexico, struggles to support fewer than thirty thousand people? Why is it that some societies view children as economic assets or liabilities while others nurture and protect them as special treasures? Why is it that in some cultures abortion is accepted as an inalienable right open to all women but in others, it is condemned as a moral outrage?

Studying population requires being sensitive to cultural differences as well as conflicting social values. It also requires recognizing the variables that define population distributions. Some are physical such as topography, soil type and quality, climates, and vegetation; some are human such as the patterns of history, economic conditions, political aspirations, and quality of life issues. Understanding the interaction of these physical and cultural influences helps explain the characteristics of human populations as well as where they are, how they got there, and what they will look like in the future.

The population explosion sparked by the Industrial Revolution in the late 1700s has placed an environmental stress on the world that some predict will surely result in the collapse of its ecosystems and the demise of the natural processes that now challenge the planet's capacity to support billions of people. Others, however, are certain that because of scientific breakthroughs, threats to the environment have diminished and the curse of global hunger has been all but eliminated. Such contradictions make population geography more speculative than predictable. While theoretical models can help explain and interpret reality, demographers can do little more than offer statistical projections about population increases and declines.

Because population growth is so fluid, it has an impact on the movement and location of people. As a result, population shifts are common thus creating new human landscapes. The natural and cultural causes for such shifts are responsible for the spatial variations in population distribution. Physical barriers such as deserts, mountain ranges, and seas play just as important a role in determining distribution and natural increase as positive cultural factors such as good harvests, stable economies, and sound trade relations, and negative ones such as war, famine, and epidemics. Add to these mobility factors, the components of fertility and life expectancy, and the importance of population geography becomes integral to understanding the fullness of human geography.

B. Focus Question to Direct Topic II Inquiry

When students have concluded their study of this topic, they should be able to prepare a comprehensive answer to this question:

Explain the characteristics, distribution, and migration of human populations on Earth's surface.

C. Key Words/Definitions

Students should be able to define the terms listed below and use each in such a way that its meaning is clear in the context of a sentence. Example:

Definition - <u>Life Expectancy</u>: the average number of years a newborn within a given population can expect to live.

Context Sentence - In today's world, immunization against such formerly fatal diseases as measles, polio, and whooping cough contributes to lowering infant mortality and increasing <u>life expectancy</u>.

Note: The citations within the parentheses next to each term identify the page numbers where it is defined and/or discussed in *Human Geography: Culture, Society, and Space*. Many terms are also included in the Glossary in Resource C.

age-sex pyramid (70)
arithmetic growth (57)
birth rate (71-72)
crude birth rate (CBR) (71)
crude death rate (CDR) (71, 73-74)
demographic transition (76-77)
demography (54, 71)
density (56)
distance decay (85)
distribution (54)
doubling time (68)
exponential growth (68)
fertility rate (as a "key issue," 55)
gravity model (82)
infant mortality (462-463)
intervening opportunity (85)
linear growth (68)
life expectancy (465)
Malthusian Theory (69)
migration (55, 81)
mortality rate (73-74, 496-499)
natural increase (71)
pull factor (83)
push factor (83)
Ravenstein's "laws" of migration (83)
stationary population level (SPL) (77)

step migration (85)
total fertility rate (TFR) (73-74)

D. Detailed Topic Outline/Text Correlation

Note: The citations within the parentheses identify the page numbers where information within the outline can be located in *Human Geography: Culture, Society, and Space.* (Seventh Edition).

II. Topic - Population

A. Geographic analysis of population (Chapter 4 on "Fundamentals of Population: Location, Distribution and Density," 53-63, provides an introductory overview of demography, its history and its present applications).
    1. Boundaries, areal units, and densities (56-58)
    2. Scale and process (77-78)
    3. Population and the environment (83)

B. Population distribution and composition
    1. Factors affecting distribution (54-55)
    2. Consequences of particular distributions (59-63)
    3. Responses to natural hazards, past, present, and future (83, 99-104)

C. Population growth and decline over time and space
    1. Historical trends and projections for the future (65-68)
    2. Regional variations in demographic transitions (76-78)
    3. Patterns of fertility, mortality, and health (71-73, 462-464)
    4. Effects of pro-natalist and anti-natalist policies (68-70)

D. Population movement
    1. Major voluntary and involuntary migrations at different scales (81-87)
    2. Short term, local movements, and activity spaces (92-97)

E. Topic II Study Questions - Population

1. Explain the difference between arithmetic growth and exponential growth.
2. What have been some of the trends in population growth and distribution since the First Agricultural Revolution?
3. What impact has the Industrial Revolution had on human populations? How have populations that have had such revolutions typically responded?
4. What is the relationship between population growth and distribution to natural hazards?
5. How does "distance decay" and "intervening opportunity" affect migration patterns?
6. What is the relationship between improvements in global health and the appearance of age-sex pyramids over the last century?
7. Why do fertility rates and mortality rates differ from region to region and sometimes even within regions?
8. What tools do demographers use to study population structures?
9. What contributions did John Snow, Thomas Malthus, and Ernst Ravenstein make to population geography?

10. Explain the demographic transition model. Why are some demographers suspect of its validity when applied to contemporary growth situations?
11. What role does medical geography play within the realm of human geography?
12. Distinguish between each of these examples of human movement:
      A. voluntary and forced migration
      B. cyclic and periodic movement
      C. immigrant and emigrant
      D. push and pull factors
13. Describe some of the pro and anti-natalist policies practiced by nations in today's world.

F. Researching Topic II - Population

Students will find that preparing short research papers (i.e., up to five pages) as part of the study of a topic is an effective means of deepening their understanding of its meaning and purpose within the realm of human geography. Such research serves not only as an introduction to the resources available about the topic but also as a strategy for applying the skills of organization and presentation essential to responding to the extended answer questions on the Advanced Placement examination in Human Geography.

The topics provided listed below serve as suggestions for the kind of research and investigation students can undertake. Each research paper should be written from an outline developed from the student's research with a brief introduction stating the hypothesis (i.e., a tentative explanation of facts tested by the investigation in the paper). A hypothesis, then, is merely a theory or a speculation that the researcher sets out to prove or disprove.

The body of the research paper provides the detail addressing the hypothesis. It provides precise information derived from the research the student has done and also follows the outline that has been prepared. As a result, the arguments should be well organized and logically presented. Including anecdotes and examples will make the paper more convincing and also more persuasive.

The final part of the research paper is the conclusion. That is the section providing a summary of what the student has argued and joins those arguments to the hypothesis. The purpose of the conclusion is to demonstrate why the hypothesis works (or does not work). It is the part of the paper where the writer rests the case.

To be convincing, research papers should contain citations and bibliographies. That gives them credibility. Such references also help validate the arguments the student presents. Because there is no *one* correct way to document research these days, teachers will provide the necessary guidance and direction for students relative to format. There are several widely used style manuals available. However, the three most often used to guide reporting research in human geography include:

American Psychological Association. *Publication Manual of the American Psychological Association*. 4th ed. Washington, D. C.: American Psychological Association. 1994.

Gibaldi, Joseph *MLA Handbook for Writers of Research Papers*. 4th ed. New York: Modern Language Association. 1995.

The Chicago Manual of Style. 14th ed. Chicago: University of Chicago Press. 1993.

Some Suggested Research Topics for Population

Malthus and Ravenstein: Comparing Two Theories of Population Geography
The Contemporary Relevance of the Demographic Transition Model
The Environmental Factors Explaining Population Distribution
China's Family Planning Program: A Demographic Case Study
National Sex Ratios: Why the Differences?
Reasons for Migration: Examining the Push and Pull Factors
Why Regional Differences in Fertility and Mortality Rates?
Using the Gravity Model to Predict Migrant Flows
National Policies Restricting Immigration: Models that Work
Trends in Global Health

G. Connecting to *Human Geography in Action*

Chapters 4 and 5 connect effectively to topics in demography and the structure of populations. Each reinforces concepts introduced in the Topic outline but there is a special emphasis on migration. Students are introduced to some of the more technical aspects of population geography in a clear and well organized way (e.g., formulae for applying the gravity model, developing scatter diagrams, using a choropleth map, etc.). In chapter 5, students learn the practical applications of age-sex pyramids in interpreting the stages of the demographic transition. Using the directions offered in chapter 4, they can also customize a model of migration flows of their own states by using digital data.

H. Sample Multiple-Choice Questions

These questions are typical of the kinds of questions students can expect on the examination in Advanced Placement Human Geography. Reviewing the section on multiple-choice questions in Chapter 1 will help students better orient themselves for selecting the appropriate answer in the sample questions included here.

Directions: Each of the questions or incomplete statements is followed by five suggested answers or completions. Select the one that is best in each case.

1. The population of Earth hovers around 6 billion people. By the year 2050, demographers project that it will reach 10 billion. Which of these reasons is primarily responsible for the present population and for the soaring growth expected over the next half century or so?

    A. Compulsory schooling provided at government expense is increasingly available to more people and that will continue to be so in the foreseeable future.

    B. Medical care and immunization are extending life expectancy for most of the world's peoples.

    C. There are more people living in cities than in rural areas with continuing urban growth a constant reality.

    D. The consistent increase in per-capita income indicates that the poverty gap is

    E. The policies of international organizations such as the United Nations and the Organization of American States encourage population growth, especially in the developed world.

2. Each year several million people from Mexico and Central America come to the United States as migrant workers generally following the harvest seasons of fruit and vegetable crops. What is the primary "push" factor that prompts them to leave their home villages?

     A. Their governments encourage such migration.

     B. There is a lack of sufficient arable land in their countries to support large-scale farming.

     C. They have not acquired the job skills necessary to work in the industries that are now dominant in their native countries.

     D. The hot, humid climate in Mexico and Central America discourages farm labor.

     E. The promise of regular work and high hourly wages that will entice them to cross the Rio Grande.

3. The population of a country divided by its area (square miles) determines its

     A. birth/death rate.

     B. rate of natural increase.

     C. population doubling time.

     D. gravity factor

     E. population density.

4. Which of the following is an historical example of an internal migration?

     A. the flight of thousands of Irish to different parts of the world as a result of the potato famine of 1848

     B. the removal of members of the Cherokee nation in 1837 and 1838 from tribal lands in Georgia to government preserves in the Oklahoma Territory

     C. the movement of people across the land bridge from Asia to North America some ten thousand years ago

     D. the African slave trade across the Middle Passage in the 1700s

     E. the Acadian diaspora from Nova Scotia in 1755 and 1788

Consider the content of the paragraph below to answer questions 5-6.

On a daily basis, more than 250,000 people are added to earth's population. Most are born in nations in the developing world. That means that one person in five lives in absolute poverty. It also is a dramatic indicator of the reality of the population explosion of the past 200 years which has been witness to a population increase from under 1 billion in 1700 to well over 6 billion predicted for the first decade of the 21st century.

5. Based on the information in the above paragraph, what is a characteristic of the developing world?

     A. low birthrates

     B. stable infant mortality rates

     C. moderate fertility rates

     D. low rates of literacy

     E. high total fertility rates (TFR)

6 . This paragraph describes conditions relating to

     A. permanent relocation.

     B. population structure.

     C. cultural determinism.

     D. demographic transition.

E. census policies.

7. What is the purpose of an age-sex pyramid?
   A. to show the spatial distribution of a population
   B. to show the migration patterns within a country
   C. to show the population structure of a country
   D. to show the fertility rate among women in the 20 to 30 age group
   E. to show the life expectancy of males and females at birth

8. Study the graph in Figure 5.8 on 78 in the text showing the Demographic Cycle. What factor most likely accounts for a country being positioned on Stage 4?
   A. improved technology and an adequate food supply
   B. significant emigration
   C. significant immigration
   D. a mass exodus or rural people to the cities
   E. war and famine

9. Which of these statements about intervening opportunity is correct?
   A. Intervening opportunity plays a major role in determining a country's population structure.
   B. Intervening opportunity is never a factor in internal migration patterns.
   C. All migration is affected by intervening opportunity.
   D. Intervening opportunity and step migration are forces that sometimes complement each other.
   E. Intervening opportunity is a phenomenon of the 20th century.

10. Study the Age-Sex Pyramids in Figure 5.4 on p. 70 and identify which countries are in the second stage of the demographic transition.
   A. Kenya and Nigeria
   B. India and Brazil
   C. Kenya and India
   D. Nigeria and Brazil
   E. All four are in stage two.

Answers: 1) B 2) B 3) E 4) B 5) E 6) B 7) C 8) A 9) D 10) E

I. Sample Free-Response Questions

These questions are similar to the free-response items likely to be on the Advanced Placement Human Geography examination.

1. Explain the position Neo-Malthusians take in arguing that what Thomas Malthus wrote about England two centuries ago can be applied to today's world, recent increases in the food supply notwithstanding.

2. Describe how the Industrial Revolution changed population trends because of the technology it introduced.

3. Analyze Ernst Ravenstein's "laws" of migration in terms of their applicability in today's world.

4. Discuss at least three factors affecting population distribution.

5. Evaluate the effectiveness of the tools demographers use to examine population trends and make predictions about future growth patterns.

Chapter 5

Advanced Placement Topic III

Cultural Patterns and Processes

Note: Questions on this topic will comprise thirteen to seventeen percent of the Advanced Placement examination. Parts Three, Four, and Ten of the text address relevant issues of Advanced Placement Topic Three. Additional information can be obtained from Part One of the text.

A. The Topic in Context - An Introduction

Because culture is so broad a topic but yet so central to the purposes of human geography, it is a challenge to keep its multiple dimensions in focus. Essentially culture is a term used to define the way a group thinks, believes and acts. But more fully, it is about what material goods a group makes and uses, and about what it values in terms of both skills and customs. And finally, it is about what a group transmits to successive generations as its legacy. What is passed on is what is treasured.

These collective habits of heart and mind reveal what a group thinks of itself as well as what it thinks of other groups. A people's culture, then, represents the totality of their world view. As a result, culture is multifaceted in that it presents the total fabric of a people's society - its structure, its governance, its language, its social and economic institutions, its arts, its traditions, and its technology. Some (like folk cultures) are simple, fragile, and all but unchanging; others (like popular cultures) are volatile, organic, and in a state of constant change.

People shape their environments through culture. They use their perceptions of space and their technology to create cultural landscapes that bear the imprint of their learned behavior. Sometimes this is done on a grand scale when societies have the technology to build great cities and create infrastructures supporting complex communication and transportation networks. But in less complicated and smaller scaled societies, when landscapes are etched with rural villages, terraced hillsides, makeshift bamboo bridges, and forest clearings serving as market towns, it is slower and more modest. But the effect is just as powerful and just as discernible.

Whether simple or complex, culture is a profound expression of the identity a group of people establishes over time. It is distinctive and often elaborate, so much so that it takes on the properties of a mosaic. Yet no culture is separate, especially in today's rapidly globalizing society. Consciously or not, every culture has borrowed from others. For human geographers, the mission is to understand the spatial expression of culture and the patterns of their distribution across Earth.

B. Focus Question to Direct Topic III Inquiry

When students have concluded their study of this topic, they should be able to prepare a comprehensive answer to this question:

Discuss the meaning of culture and explain how cultures distribute themselves across Earth.

C. Key Words/Definitions

Students should be able to define these terms and use each in such a way that its meaning is clear in the context of a sentence. Example:

Definition - <u>Diffusion:</u> the spreading of elements of culture (e.g., ideas, technologies, and products) among many peoples.

Context Sentence - Even though the internet was developed for military purposes by the Department of Defense, its <u>diffusion</u> has been so comprehensive that it is now a part of virtually every culture in the world.

Note: The citations within the parentheses next to each term identify the pages where it is defined and/or discussed in *Human Geography: Culture, Society, and Space* (Seventh Edition). Many terms are also included in the Glossary in Resource C.

acculturation (29, 486)
animism (164)
conquest and agricultural theories (128)
contagious diffusion (28)
cultural diffusion (27-29)
cultural environments (32-33)
cultural landscape (24-25)
cultural perception (29-32)
culture (21-22)
culture hearths (25-27)
culture realms (22)
culture regions (22)
culture traits (22)
folk culture (441)
gender gap (493-508)
multilingualism (141-146)
popular culture (441)
racism (482-483)
standard language (113)

D. Detailed Topic Outline/Text Correlation

Note: The citations within the parentheses identify where information within the outline can be located in *Human Geography: Culture, Society, and Space* (Seventh Edition).

Topic III - Cultural Patterns and Processes

A. Concepts of Culture
    1. Traits and complexes (17)
    2. Diffusion (27-29)
    3. Acculturation (29)
    4. Cultural regions and realms (16-18, 22, 29-31)

B. Cultural Differences

1. Language (Part 3 on "The Global Linguistics Mosaic" is a detailed treatment of the geography of language and its connection to culture. Each of the chapters deserves careful study.)

2. Religion (Part 4 on "The Geography of Religion" provides a comprehensive treatment of the world's major belief systems. Special attention should be paid to the discussion of cultural landscapes as they relate to Buddhism (169-170), Chinese religions (170-171), Judaism (171-172), Christianity (172-175), Islam (175-179) and Hinduism (167-169).

3. Ethnicity (483-492) (The discussion on human biological variation, genentic diseases on pages 476-478 and race in "The Geography of Race" on   480-482 and 504-508 places ethnicity in a meaningful context.)

4. Gender (494-495)

C. Environmental impact and cultural attitudes and practices (500-504)

D. Cultural landscapes and cultural identity
    1. Values and preferences (504-508)
    2. Symbolic landscapes and sense of place (485)

E. Topic III Study Questions - Cultural Patterns and Processes

1. Define culture. Provide some examples explaining the processes of cultural diffusion.
2. Why is the mosaic of language and religion of interest and value to the cultural geographer?
3. What are the major components that make up the definition of language?
4. What is a standard language?
5. Study the language map of Europe (Figure 8.3, p. 116) and explain how it is a diffusion model.
6. What are some of the theories of language diffusion? What analysis has Colin Renfrew, the British scholar, brought to the interpretation of the search for the source for a "superfamily" of languages?
7. What is toponomy? What does it reveal about the culture of a place?
8. Why are place names categorized?
9. Define religion. What are some of the ways religions manifest themselves within a culture?
10. Where are the source areas of the world's major belief systems? Explain how they were diffused.
11. Provide examples to explain the differences between global and regional religions.
12. What is secularization? Why is it a topic of inquiry for human geographers?
13. Describe some of the cultural dimensions of some key gender issues that have geographic implications.
14. Describe how a cultural landscape can also be a symbolic landscape. Explain how such landscapes relate to popular and folk culture.
15. Provide some examples illustrating how culture and environment interact. Assess some positive and negative aspects of that interaction.

F. Researching Topic III - Cultural Patterns and Processes

Students will find that preparing short research papers (i.e., up to five pages) as part of the study of a topic is an effective means of deepening their understanding of its meaning and purpose within the realm of human geography. Such research serves not only as an introduction to the resources available about the topic but also as a strategy for applying the skills of organization and presentation essential to responding to the extended answer questions on the Advanced Placement examination in Human Geography.

The topics listed below serve as suggestions for the kind of research and investigation students can undertake. Each research paper should be written from an outline developed from the student's research with a brief introduction stating the hypothesis (i.e., a tentative explanation of facts tested by the investigation in the paper). A hypothesis, then, is merely a theory or a speculation that the researcher sets out to prove or disprove.

The body of the research paper provides the detail addressing the hypothesis. It provides precise information derived from the research the student has done and also follows the outline that has been prepared. As a result, the arguments should be well organized and logically presented. Including anecdotes and examples will make the paper more convincing and also more persuasive.

The final part of the research paper is the conclusion. That is the section providing a summary of what the student has argued and joins those arguments to the hypothesis. The purpose of the conclusion is to demonstrate why the hypothesis works (or does not work). It is the part of the paper where the writer rests the case.

To be convincing, research papers should contain citations and bibliographies. That gives them credibility. Such references also help validate the arguments the student presents. Because there is no *one* correct way to document research these days, teachers will provide the necessary guidance and direction for students relative to format. There are several widely used style manuals available. However, the three most often used to guide reporting research in human geography include:

American Psychological Association. *Publication Manual of the American Psychological Association*. 4th ed. Washington, D. C.: American Psychological Association. 1994.

Gibaldi, Joseph *MLA Handbook for Writers of Research Papers*. 4th ed. New York: Modern Language Association. 1995.

The Chicago Manual of Style. 14th ed. Chicago: University of Chicago Press. 1993.

Some Suggested Research Topics for Cultural Patterns and Processes

Reading Cultural Landscapes: A Geographic Perspective
Culture and the Physical Environment: How They Interact
Language as a Descriptor of Region
Religion as a Descriptor of Region
The Why? and Where? of "Official" Languages
Language as a Nation Builder
The Global Diffusion of European Culture: A Case Study
Religion and the Geography of Diet
Looking at a Religious Landscape: A Case Study
Reading Cultural Landscapes: A Geographic Perspective

G. Connecting to *Human Geography in Action*

The components of cultural geography are addressed in several places in the book. One especially helpful activity is in Chapter 2, Part III on "Regional Imagery." on 2-15. It suggests some strategies for developing a clearer understanding of cultural landscapes and their purpose. The setting is the American southwest.

Chapter 11, Part I on 11-7 to 11-9 is a mapping exercise that graphically illustrates the applications of diffusion. Northern Ireland is the model used to illustrate the process. Both activities are CD-based. In addition, the chapters in which each appears concludes with a helpful bibliography for further reading in topics in cultural geography.

H. Sample Multiple Choice Questions

These questions are typical of the kinds of questions students can expect on the examination in Advanced Placement Human Geography. Reviewing the section on multiple-choice questions in Chapter 1 will help students better orient themselves for selecting the appropriate answer in the sample questions included here.

Directions: Each of the questions or incomplete statements is followed by five suggested answers or completions. Select the one that is best in each case.

1. National flags within a region often share common designs but in different colors and scales. The flags of Scandinavia are a good example. What is the symbol found on the flags of these countries that is a mark of their cultural identity?
   A. a five pointed star
   B. a two edged sword
   C. a Latin cross
   D. a gold crescent
   E. a darkened oval

2. Which of these statements is most accurate in its interpretation of the role gender plays in geography?
   A. Demographic statistics for developing countries (almost always reported in the aggregate) tend to conceal gender gaps.
   B. Modernization and economic development have given most women equal status with men.
   C. Economics is the primary determinant of the role of women in a society.
   D. In the developing world, the number of women in the work force has declined in recent years.
   E. Because of increased public awareness worldwide about the role women play in society, their quality of life and working conditions have improved significantly in every region of the world since 1950.

3. Which one of these newspaper headlines illustrates the diffusion process?
   A. Swine Flu Outbreak Reaches Crisis Level
   B. Japanese Rice Consumption on the Increase
   C. Car Makers Pledge Improved Gas Mileage
   D. Wheat Prices Stable Since July
   E. Civil War Imminent in Taris Republic

4. Which of these is an example of a culture trait?
   A. sleeping

B. eating a meal
C. wearing a turban
D. taking a morning walk
E. parenting

5. Which of these is an example of a cultural landscape?
   A. a coastal wetland
   B. a cloud forest
   C. wadis in a sandy desert
   D. a stand of mangrove trees
   E. a park area off an interstate

6. A people who are part of a culture that does not have a written language are said to be
   A. illiterate.
   B. preliterate.
   C. symbolic.
   D. derivative.
   E. prehistoric.

7. Which of these characteristics is shared by all languages?
   A. static and constant
   B. distinct and separate
   C. non-symbolic
   D. changing and mutable
   E. based on a written alphabet

8. Which of these inventions had the greatest impact on standardizing languages worldwide?
   A. the moldboard plow
   B. the printing press
   C. the cathode ray tube
   D. the smallpox vaccine
   E. the internal combustion engine

9. Which of these statement about gender and religion is true.
   A. All religions promote a division of labor based on gender.
   B. There is little evidence on any cultural landscape of differences between the sexes.
   C. In many societies, religion has relegated women to an inferior status.
   D. Most of the world's religions encourage gender equity.
   E. Social roles based on gender exist only in animistic religions.

10. All of the following are indicators of a group's culture except their.
    A. land-use practices.
    B. patterns of speech.
    C. methods of conflict resolution.
    D. systems of trade.
    E. ability to speak a language.

Answers: 1) C 2) A 3) A 4) C 5) E 6) B 7) D 8) B 9) C 10) E

I. Sample Free-Response Questions

These questions are similar to the free-response items likely to be on the Advanced Placement Human Geography examination.

1. Explain the processes by which languages change. Why do such changes make the spatial search for language origins so problematic?

2. Describe the relationship between language and culture. Provide at least two examples.

3. Compare the diffusion of Christianity and Islam. Explain how the processes of diffusion contributed to making each a global religion.

4. Explain the role sequent occupancy plays in transforming cultural landscapes. Use animistic religion as an indicator.

5. Explain how culture helps shape the characteristics of a region.

Chapter 6

Advanced Placement Topic IV

Political Organization of Space

Note: Questions on this topic comprise thirteen to seventeen percent of the Advanced Placement examination. Part Five of the text relates most closely to the preparatory information needed for Topic Four of the Advanced Placement test.

A. The Topic in Context: An Introduction

Like it or not, politics is one of the realities of modern life. Not only is it an expression of a philosophy of government about how to conduct public business, but it also helps define the boundaries of places within which people live. In fact, that has been the case since the times of the earliest hunting and gathering societies. With the same authority and insistence that contemporary sovereign states exhaustively partition their territory, those ancient groups were just as manipulative. They staked their claims on regions where they could take game, catch fish, dig for roots, and harvest fruits and nuts. Only the scale and complexity of the extent of the two groups' ambitions differ. Past or present, the lesson is that territory and its governance is the power source of politics.

Through whatever governments they establish to exercise such power, people partition space for a variety of reasons. Some are motivated to create culture enclaves recognizing a common history, language, religion, and set of economic priorities; some to establish control advancing a particular social or political ideology; some to preserve an ethnic or racial identity; some to acquire more and more land area for the resources and trade opportunity it offers; and still others to increase their prestige and dominance through the development of colonies. Understandably, these efforts to divide Earth into political segments over which governments have authority are the source both cooperation and conflict. That means the relationship between and among nations is sometimes serene, sometimes strained, sometimes disruptive, but always fragile. Thus Earth's surface is ever being divided, unified, organized, and reorganized through negotiation, war, cession, and purchase.

Enter political geography. Its purpose is to explain the processes of change resulting from the constantly evolving relationships among the world's nations. It explains what boundaries exist, where they are, the policies governments develop defining their relationships with other powers, and the alliance systems they develop to promote and protect their own interests.

But as important as international relations are, political geographers recognize that political activities on a local scale have a special importance as well. Fierce debates often develop over the interpretation of census data used to delineate ward boundaries in cities and towns or the size and shape of representative districts within a state, province, or prefecture. Such arguments are almost always partisan and almost always result in gerrymandered configurations that reflect the give and take of compromise. The shape of such local entities like the shape of nation-states themselves may reflect the ability of governmental units to manage and consolidate territory. Even though a circle would be the most efficient political shape, such a compact territorial expression is as unrealistic as it is impossible, especially since the distribution of topographic features may produce physical barriers that limit the ability to govern. What remains, then, is a collection of imperfect political units - some large, some small, some symmetrical, some misshapen - that constitute the organizing territorial principal of human activities.

In the modern world where societies are technologically oriented and economies centered on service industries, the older notions of political geography as the study of a collection of sovereign units is in transformation. Today political geographers study not only local, regional, and national spatial arrangements, but also international and supranational alliance systems. These new organizational models transcend the nation-state system that has traditionally defined the world order since the end of the Middle Ages. In the current web of complex economic, military, and cultural relationships that characterize how nations presently interact, the old framework is often inadequate in dealing with the issues and problems that involve countries across the regions of the world. The extraction, distribution and pricing of petroleum is a convincing illustration of the necessity of alliance networks ensuring the availability to oil and oil products where they are needed across the globe at competitive but affordable prices.

Understanding political geography helps make sense of the interlocking systems that join, divide, and section Earth's space. Indeed political geography influences every dimension of people's lives from voting patterns and travel preferences to trade options and the consumption of goods and the use of services. Political units and the boundaries that define them constitute the divisions of the world that are locally managed and controlled but globally interconnected and interdependent.

B. Focus Question to Direct Topic IV Inquiry

When students have concluded the study of this topic, they should be able to prepare a comprehensive answer to this question:

Discuss how the forces of cooperation and conflict among the world's political units influence the division and control of Earth's surface.

C. Key Words/Definitions

Students should be able to define these terms and use each in such a way that its meaning is clear in the context of a sentence. Example:

Definition - Balkanization: the process by which a region is fragmented into smaller states which are generally hostile political units.

Context Sentence - After the breakup of the Soviet Union in 1991-92, the balkanization of some of the former republics - especially in the Caucuses region - was so destructive to internal harmony that it brought them to the brink economic collapse.

Note: The citations within the parentheses next to each term identify the pages where it is defined and/or discussed in *Human Geography: Culture, Society, and Space* (Seventh Edition). Many terms are also included in the Glossary in Resource C .

alliance system (237-239)
balkanization (252, 257-261)
boundaries (211-212, 214-216)
centrifugal forces (231-232)
centripetal forces (232-233)
colonialism (220-221)
compact state (210)
demarcation (212)

devolution (252, 257-261)
elongated state (210)
enclave (211)
ethnic conflict (253-256)
exclave (211)
federal system (228)
frontier (214)
geopolitics (224)
gerrymander (231)
Heartland Theory (224-226)
imperialism (220-221)
irredentism (Reference section)
microstate (210)
nation-state (204, 208-209)
nationalism (215)
perforated state (210)
prorupt state (210)
Rimland Theory (224-226)
secular state (164)
sovereignty (204, 208-209)
state (204)
stateless nations (205)
supranationalism (235, 244-245, 247-249)
territoriality (203)
theocracy (202)
tribalism (232-233)
unitary system (228)

D. Detailed Topic Outline/Text Correlation

Note: The citations within the parentheses identify where information within the outline can be located in *Human Geography: Culture, Society, and Space* (Seventh Edition).

Topic IV - Political organization of Space

A. Nature and significance of political boundaries
    1. Ways of conceptualizing territory: from local to global (209-211)
    2. Influence of boundaries on group identity and political representation (211)

B. Evolution of the contemporary political pattern
    1. Territorial assumptions underlying the nation-state ideal (Reference section, 204, 208-209)
    2. Colonialism and imperialism (220-221.) While there is no single section discussing imperialism in the text, there is a good contextual discussion that explores its ramifications in several regions of the world through an analysis of the boundaries between major religions. Refer to pages 181-190 as an illustration.
    3. Internal political boundaries and arrangements (228)

C. Challenges to inherited political-territorial arrangements
    1. Changing nature of sovereignty (204, 208-109)
    2. Fragmentation, unification, alliance (235, 244-245, 247-249)

3. Spatial relationships between political patterns and patterns of ethnicity, economy, and environment (253-256)

E. Topic IV Study Questions - Political Organization of Space

1. What is political geography?
2. Why is the traditional notion of the nation-state concept presently in transition?
3. Define sovereignty. How is it manifest among the members of the family of nations?
4. Distinguish between the meaning of "country" and "nation-state."
5. In what sense are boundaries at the core of the inquiries conducted by political geographers? Identify types of boundaries and their function.
6. How are cooperation and conflict involved in influencing the distribution of social, political, and economic spaces on Earth at different scales?
7. What is the impact of multiple spatial divisions on peoples lives (e.g., school districts, congressional districts, suburban subdivisions, state and country boundaries, free trade zones etc.)?
8. What are some of the causes of border conflicts and internal territorial disputes? Provide some examples (either current or historical).
9. How do differing points of view play a role in disputes that develop over territory and resources?
10. How does a nation's shape affect both issues of governance and the development of its foreign policy?
11. How can developments such as new technologies and new markets act as change agents in a region?
12. How have colonialism and imperialism been both constructive and disruptive forces in the era since the Age of European Exploration in the sixteenth and seventeenth centuries?
13. How can efforts at religious conversion through missionary activities cause political and cultural conflict in an area?. How does it relate to the changing nature of sovereignty?
14. What are some of the forms that supranationalism takes in the contemporary world?

F. Researching Topic IV - Political Organization of Space

Students will find that preparing short research papers (i.e., up to five pages) as part of the study of a topic is an effective means of deepening their understanding of its meaning and purpose within the realm of human geography. Such research serves not only as an introduction to the resources available about the topic but also as a strategy for applying the skills of organization and presentation essential to responding to the extended answer questions on the Advanced Placement examination in Human Geography.

The topics listed below serve as suggestions for the kind of research and investigation students can undertake. Each research paper should be written from an outline developed from the student's research with a brief introduction stating the hypothesis (i.e., a tentative explanation of facts tested by the investigation in the paper). A hypothesis, then, is merely a theory or a speculation that the researcher sets out to prove or disprove.

The body of the research paper provides the detail addressing the hypothesis. It presents precise information derived from the research the student has done and also follows the outline that has been prepared. As a result, the arguments should be well organized and logically presented. Including anecdotes and examples will make the paper more convincing and also more persuasive.

The final part of the research paper is the conclusion. That is the section providing a summary of what the student has argued and joins those arguments to the hypothesis. The purpose of the conclusion is to demonstrate why the hypothesis works (or does not work). It is the part of the paper where the writer rests the case.

To be convincing, research papers should contain citations and bibliographies. That gives them credibility. Such references also help validate the arguments the student presents. Because there is no *one* correct way to document research these days, teachers will provide the necessary guidance and direction for students relative to format. There are several widely used style manuals available. However, the three most often used to guide reporting research in human geography include:

American Psychological Association. *Publication Manual of the American Psychological Association*. 4th ed. Washington, D. C.: American Psychological Association. 1994.

Gibaldi, Joseph *MLA Handbook for Writers of Research Papers*. 4th ed. New York: Modern Language Association. 1995.

The Chicago Manual of Style. 14th ed. Chicago: University of Chicago Press. 1993.

Some Suggested Research Topics for the Political Organization of Space

The Idea of the Nation
Heartland v. Rimland: Are They Theories in Conflict?
The Shapes of Countries: Do They Make a Difference?
Political Insulation: North Korea as a Case Study
Making Frontiers into Boundaries: Some Historical Examples
Geopolitics: Myth or Reality?
World Order as a Political Concept: Designing a Definition
Colonialism and the Process of Enculturation
Balancing Power: The States and the Federal Government - The American Experience
The European Union: A Case Study in Supranationalism

G. Connecting to *Human Geography in Action*

Chapter 12 on "The Rise of Nationalism and the Fall of Yugoslavia" offers a compelling case study illustrating the role political geography plays in the realignment of boundaries. Many of the concepts presented in the topic outline for this unit of study is applied in the reconfiguring of the former Yugoslavia. Map and data analysis are important components of the chapter and challenge students to "unlearn" the definitions of many political terms that are being changed and reinterpreted due to events in the international community since the end of the Cold War in 1991.

H. Sample Multiple-Choice Questions

These questions are typical of the kinds of questions students can expect on the examination in Advanced Placement Human Geography. Reviewing the section on multiple-choice questions in Chapter 1 will help students better orient themselves for selecting the appropriate answer in the sample questions included here.

Directions: Each of the questions or incomplete statements is followed by five suggested answers or completions. Select the one that is best in each case.

1. Which of the following is an example of a physical-political international boundary?
    A. railroad
    B. river
    C. canal
    D. meridian
    E. rainforest

2. All of the following are terms that connote the concept of a nation-state except
    A. linguistic.
    B. religious.
    C. ethnic.
    D. racial.
    E. political.

3. Use your mental map to classify the boundaries that define Colorado.
    A. superimposed
    B. antecedent
    C. cultural-political
    D. geometric
    E. relict

4. Why are capital cities of interest to political geographers?
    A. They are core areas always centrally located in the heart of a state.
    B. They are forward cities designed to promote their countries' political and economic objectives.
    C. Typically capital cities symbolize the cultural and historic identity of their countries.
    D. They are primarily centers of government power without any other urban functions.
    E. They are unstable governmental units that are constantly being moved to serve some special political objective.

5. Which of the following is an example of a centripetal force designed to promote national unity?
    A. an interstate highway system constructed as a military road network
    B. an educational program promoted by an ethnic group establishing its cultural dominance in a region
    C. a plan to establish a national language in a multicultural society
    D. a relocation policy to move recent immigrants to a country's underdeveloped physical regions
    E. a wall built around the capital city of a country to set it apart as a special place

6. Which statement best describes Mackinder's Heartland Theory?
    A. It proposed land-based power rather than ocean dominance as the determining factor in ruling the world.
    B. It established that a multipolar world will ensure shared power among nations.
    C. It hypothesized that because centripetal forces seldom counterbalance centrifugal forces, conflict within the international community is a constant reality.

D. It concluded that a pivot area in the center of a landmass will always be the key factor in making a nation globally dominant.

E. It argued that regardless of a nation's location, power would always be determined by the abundance of its natural resources.

7. Supranational organizations have become a contemporary reality largely because
   A. the state system is an inadequate instrument for dealing with world issues and problems.
   B. the collapse of the Soviet Union and the end of the Cold War has increased polarization among nation-states.
   C. nations must act unilaterally if they are to achieve their goals.
   D. nations in the developed realm need a power base to check the ambitions of nations in the developing realm.
   E. a world government is essential if there is to be international peace.

8. Political geographers argue that progress toward a unified Europe depends on
   A. agreements on refugee and displaced persons questions.
   B. the elimination of current national boundaries.
   C. a system of military alliances.
   D. the establishment of a common and stable currency.
   E. a modernized transportation network unifying the region.

9. What best characterizes the purpose of the North Atlantic Treaty Organization (NATO)?
   A. a military alliance
   B. an international peace organization
   C. an international court
   D. a nonpartisan political organization
   E. a regional economic union

10. When a country succumbs to devolutionary forces, it
    A. tends to grow stronger and more unified.
    B. develops a rapidly expanding economy.
    C. suffers a significant reduction in its population.
    D. divides along regional lines.
    E. responds to the power of centripetal forces.

Answers: 1) B 2) E 3) D 4) C 5) A 6) D 7)A 8) D 9) A 10) D

I. Sample Free-Response Questions

These questions are similar to the free-response items likely to be on the Advanced Placement Human Geography examination.

1. Contrast the unitary state model with the federal model. Identify the unifying and divisive forces of each.

2. Discuss the genetic boundary classification pioneered by Richard Hartshorne.

3. Explain why supranational alliances exist in the modern world. Provide some examples illustrating the point of the answer.

4. Assess the importance of centripetal forces as factors in unifying a political unit.

5. Describe the devolutionary process and explain how it has affected particular European countries.

Chapter 7

Advanced Placement Topic V

Agricultural and Rural Land Use

Note: Questions on this topic will comprise thirteen to seventeen percent of the Advanced Placement examination. Part Six of the text relates most closely to information required for Advanced Placement Topic Five.

A. The Topic in Context - An Introduction

Deep in the preliterate world of hunting and gathering, some group in some unidentified place learned - probably quite by accident - the miracle of agriculture. Its members discovered that by the deliberate tending of crops and livestock, they could provide a far more reliable food supply than what tracking wild animals, grubbing for fruits and berries, and digging for roots had to offer.

But the discovery was not confined to a single place. Rather, agriculture emerged sequentially in several regions of the world, all of which were defined by fertile soil, a moderate climate, and the availability of a reliable water supply. As a result, some 12,000 years ago, a pattern of farming activity had developed in the river valleys of the Nile, the Tigris and Euphrates, the Indus, and the Yellow (Huang He) in eastern China. The age of food producers had begun. What resulted were permanent settlements, significant population increases, the invention of written languages, and complex government structures built on an extensive system of divisions of labor.

More than any other human activity, agriculture changed Earth's cultural landscape in ways that have not only transformed the way people live but also make it possible for billions of them to successfully inhabit today's world. Unlike other transformations, however, agriculture developed in several stages. Historians and human geographers call these *revolutions* because they wrought changes that have had a deep and enduring impact on both life styles and settlement patterns. To date, there have been three of these revolutions, each dramatic but shaping, and each complicated but consequential. The first achieved plant and animal domestication, a global process that took thousand of years to accomplish; the second, centered in Europe during the Middle Ages and prelude to the Industrial Revolution, involved improved methods of cultivating, producing and storing food; and the third called the Green Revolution is still in progress. Using sophisticated technology and research into the genetic make-up of food commodities, this revolution has increased crop yields to support the demands of a soaring world population. Without the success of this revolution, global famine would be as much a reality and as devastating as both epidemics and nuclear war.

Human geographers examine agricultural and rural land use in order to understand the disparities in the world production and distribution of food. They also study the reasons for overproduction in some regions and underproduction in others. Understanding the complex environmental and technological reasons for these inequities provides a frame of reference for finding solutions to providing food supplies on a more fair basis for all the world. But certain factors are beyond their control. These involve the often perplexing patterns of trade and the uncertainty of the world's markets as well as conflicts between poor farmers with little land and rich ones with great aggregates of acreage.

Among the tools human geographers use to aid in their understanding of the positive and negative aspects of the patterns of agricultural production is the spatial model. Even though these models are idealized representations of reality, nonetheless they simplify the complex and facilitate the search for solutions. The Von Thünen's Spatial Model of Farming is an example. Even though several centuries old, it still has application, and continues to be central to the study of rural geography.

Much of Earth's surface is devoted to agricultural activity. Over the millennia, it has created cultural landscapes that have changed all the world's regions. Rolling wheat lands in North America, Australia, Argentina, and on the Ukrainian steppes to terraced hill slopes in Asia to slash and burn patches in Amazonia testify to the extent of farming. Human geography examines all the factors that continually challenge the ability of farmers to secure an adequate food supply and accommodate to the fragile balance between supply and demand on a global scale.

B. Focus Question to Direct Topic V Inquiry

When students have concluded their study of this topic, they should be able to prepare a comprehensive answer to this question:

Describe how the Von Thünen Model of Farming developed in early nineteenth century Europe helps explain rural spatial patterns common to the First and Second Agricultural Revolutions as well as to those resulting from the Third Agricultural Revolution.

C. Key Words/Definitions

Students should be able to define these terms and use each in such a way that its meaning is clear in the context of a sentence. Example:

Definition - <u>Wattle</u>: construction processes used in traditional buildings employing poles intertwined tightly with twigs, reeds, or branches, and then plastered with mud; used for walls, fences and other enclosures, and roofs

Context Sentence - <u>Wattle</u> buildings are common sights on the rural landscapes of Southeast Asia because of the ample availability of the materials used in the construction of such structures.

Note: The citations within the parentheses next to each term identify where it is defined and/or discussed in *Human Geography: Culture, Society, and Space.* (Seventh Edition) Many terms are also included in the Glossary in Resource C.

agribusiness (309)
agriculture (273)
Agricultural Revolutions
      • First/Neolithic (276)
      • Second (282)
      • Third (284, 309)
      • Green Revolution (307)
commercial/industrial agriculture (300)
cultural landscape (302-303)
diffusion (293)
      • diffusion routes (293)

• maladaptive diffusion (295)
dispersed settlement (286)
domestication
     • animal (279)
     • plant (277)
economic activities
     • primary (272)
     • secondary (273)
     • tertiary (273)
extractive economic activity (272)
hamlet (294)
nucleated/agglomerated settlement (287)
paleolithic (Reference section)
shifting cultivation (280)
subsistence farming (280-281)
Thünian patterns (283)
traditional architecture (290-293)
village (294)
Von Thünen's Spatial Model of Farming/Von Thünen's Model of Agricultural Location (283)

D. Detailed Topic Outline/Text Correlation

Note: The citations within the parentheses identify where information within the outline can be located in *Human Geography: Culture, Society, and Space* (Seventh Edition).

Topic V. Agricultural and Rural Land Use

A. Development and diffusion of agriculture
     1. First/Neolithic Agricultural Revolution (276)
     2. Evolution of energy sources and technology (272-273)
     3. Regions of plant and animal domestication (277)

B. Major agricultural production regions
     1. Agricultural systems associated with major bio-climatic zones (302-303)
     2. Production and food supply: linkages and flows (293-295)

C. Rural land use and change
     1. Location and land use models (Examine the Von Thünen Model (283) and the achievements of the three agricultural revolutions, (276-309)
     2. Intensification and land use (Table 8.1 on page 278, 277)
     3. Settlement systems (287)

D. Impacts of modern agricultural change
     1. Green Revolution (307)
     2. Consumption, nutrition, and hunger (Chapter 30)
     3. Industrial/commercial agriculture (300)
     4. Environmental change (530): desertification (535-537), deforestation (307, 535-537), farmland loss to urban growth (437, 460-461), greenhouse warming effect (516), acid rain (535)

E. Topic V Study Questions - Agricultural and Rural Land Use

1. Describe the difference between paleolithic and neolithic societies.
2. What role did fire and metallurgy play in hunting and gathering societies and in early agricultural communities?
3. Why are fishing and lumbering included in the study of agricultural geography?
4. What is the significance of the First Agricultural Revolution?
5. Describe the three levels of economic activities that show the range from simple to complex and from ancient practices to modern ones..
6. Why is agriculture classified as a part of the extractive sector in the hierarchy of economic activities?
7. What is subsistence agriculture? In what regions of today's world does it still prevail?
8. Explain the relationship between plant and animal domestication and agricultural practice.
9. Describe some of the practical alternatives to subsistence agriculture.
10. Identify the Second Agricultural Revolution. How did it differ from the First Agricultural Revolution?
11. What is the nature of the Third Agricultural Revolution (which is still in progress)? Why is it also identified as the Green Revolution?
12. Discuss Von Thünen's Model of Farming. Relate the model to soil quality and climate changes.
13. Why are human geographers interested in the nature of human settlement?
14. Distinguish between dispersed and nucleated settlements.
15. Explain how the forms, functions, materials, and spacing of rural dwellings (and settlements) reveal a great deal about a region and its culture. How are these manifestations of human/environmental interaction?
16. Describe commercial agriculture. What is the relationship between the development of commercial agriculture and European colonial policy over the last two centuries?
17. What conclusions can be drawn about the patterns of world agriculture by studying page 282?
18. Assess the impact of changing agricultural practices in (a) North America. (b) Latin America, and (c) Africa.
19. Describe some of the risks implicit in single crop economies.
20. Explain why the global network of farm production is more responsive to the needs of the urbanized societies of the industrialized democracies in the developed world than to more marginal societies in the developing world.

F. Researching Topic V - Agricultural and Rural Land Use

Students will find that preparing short research papers (i.e., up to five pages) as part of the study of a topic is an effective means of deepening their understanding of its meaning and purpose within the realm of human geography. Such research serves not only as an introduction to the resources available about the topic but also as a strategy for applying the skills of organization and presentation essential to responding to the extended answer questions on the Advanced Placement examination in Human Geography.

The topics provided here are certainly not comprehensive and all-inclusive, but only serve as suggestions for the kind of research and investigation students can undertake. Each research paper should be written from an outline developed from the student's research with a brief introduction stating the hypothesis (i.e., a tentative explanation that accounts for a set of facts that will be tested by the investigation presented in the paper). A hypothesis, then, is merely a theory or a speculation that the researcher sets out to prove or disprove.

The body of the research paper provides the detail addressing the hypothesis. It provides precise information derived from the research the student has done and also follows the outline that has been prepared. As a result, the arguments should be well organized and logically presented. Including anecdotes and examples will make the paper more convincing and also more persuasive.

The final part of the research paper is the conclusion. That is the section providing a summary of what the student has argued and joins those arguments to the hypothesis. The purpose of the conclusion is to demonstrate why the hypothesis works (or does not work). It is the part of the paper where the writer rests the case.

To be convincing, research papers should contain citations and bibliographies. That gives them credibility and it also helps validate the arguments the student presents. Because there is no *one* correct way to document research these days, teachers will provide the necessary guidance and direction for students There are several widely used style manuals available. However, the three most often used to guide reporting research in human geography include:

American Psychological Association. *Publication Manual of the American Psychological Association*. 4th ed. Washington, D. C.: American Psychological Association. 1994.

Gibaldi, Joseph *MLA Handbook for Writers of Research Papers*. 4th ed. New York: Modern Language Association. 1995.

The Chicago Manual of Style. 14th ed. Chicago: University of Chicago Press. 1993.

Some Suggested Research Topics for Agricultural and Rural Land Use

Thomas Malthus and the Malthusian Equation: An Evaluation
The World's Principal Food Crops: Their Distributions and Their Markets
Factors Influencing Land Use: Examining Models as Production Determinants
The Green Revolution and Problems of Increasing Food Production
International Law and the Regulation of the World's Fishing Areas
In Search of New Technologies: Aquaculture and the Use of Hybrids
Barriers to Increasing Agricultural Production in the Developing World
Wheat and Rice as Cultural Indicators: A Case Study
Modernization and Changing Residential Traditions in Rural Settlements
The Three Agricultural Revolutions: A Contrast in the Study of Spatial Settings

G. Connecting to *Human Geography in Action*

Chapter 13 (13-1 to 13-24) examines the ways humans can have an impact on the environment. It connects them to the primary, secondary, and tertiary sectors of the economy as a means of providing a realistic context. The emphasis is on the positive and negative results of environmental change. Thus, students are challenged to examine the causal relationships affecting people and their environments. The chapter has a strong agricultural orientation and complements virtually every aspect of Topic V.

H. Sample Multiple-Choice Questions

These questions are typical of the kinds of questions students can expect on the examination in Advanced Placement Human Geography. Reviewing the section on multiple-choice questions in Chapter 1 will help students better orient themselves for selecting the appropriate answer in the sample questions included here.

Directions: Each of the questions or incomplete statements is followed by five suggested answers or completions. Select the one that is best in each case.

1. What is the hypothesis relating to food production and agriculture that Thomas Malthus established in his essay on population?
    A. There are no controls available to limit population growth.
    B. Food production increases arithmetically as population increases geometrically.
    C. The positive checks on population growth are war, famine, and disease.
    D. Government policy is the only effective control on population growth.
    E. Earth's capacity to produce food consistently outruns natural increases in the population.

2. Von Thünen's spatial model of farming is predicated on what theoretical construct?
    A. concentric rings
    B. irregular distribution patterns
    C. linear distributions
    D. interrelated stages of development
    E changing residential styles

3. Which of the following is an example of a nucleated settlement pattern?
    A. Villages are located along a narrow road at approximately half mile intervals.
    B. People live in widely scattered and ill-formed settlements.
    C. Houses and other buildings are grouped in clusters.
    D. Settlements are singly on small plots where there are no dwellings or out buildings.
    E. Human activity follows a consistent but irregular distribution pattern.

4. Which of the following is illustrative of maladaptive diffusion?
    A. a teepee on the prairies of North America
    B. a yurt on the Mongolian steppe
    C. a ranch house in New Mexico
    D. a three decker apartment building in an urban neighborhood in Worcester, MA
    E. a Phoenix subdivision comprised of Cape Cod style houses

5. How do human geographers identify the smallest cluster of houses and non-residential buildings?
    A. as a village
    B. as a town
    C. as a hamlet
    D. as a cooperative
    E. as a borough

6. Identify the primary cause of the Third Agricultural Revolution.
    A. crop diversification

B. global warming

C. government subsidies

D. biotechnology

E. success at stabilizing the world's population

7. What is the general location of the largest areas of commercial farms?

A. in tropical zones

B. in North America

C. in the temperate zones

D. in the countries of the former Soviet Union

E. in Subsaharan Africa

8. The primary reason for the increased success of agriculture on a global scale global is directly related to

A. the decisions of the United Nations Security Council and General Assembly.

B. the policies of the United States Department of Agriculture.

C. the worldwide commercialization of farming.

D. the recent advances in technology and genetic engineering.

E. the decline in subsistence farming and slash and burn techniques.

9. The processes of shifting cultivation most directly relates to

A. the First Agricultural Revolution.

B. the Second Agricultural Revolution.

C. The Green Revolution.

D. hunting and gathering economies.

E. subsistence farming.

10. Which of the following is an example of a tertiary economic activity?

A. forestry, lumbering, and mining

B. herding, hunting, and gathering

C. manufacturing chemical fertilizers

D. working in a service industry

E. commercial wheat cultivation

Answers: 1) B 2) A 3) C 4) E 5) C 6) D 7) C 8) D 9) E 10) D

I. Sample Free-Response Questions

These questions are similar to the free-response items likely to be on the Advanced Placement Human Geography examination.

1. To answer this question, refer to pages 303-304 in the text. Compare the climatic relationships in similar crop-growing areas around the world. Explain the reasons for the relationships you observe.

2. Explain how each of the three agricultural revolutions affected food production in their respective historical periods.

3. Describe the relationships that exist between housing styles and the physical environment. What accounts for such phenomena as maladaptive diffusion?

4. Discuss how European colonialism was responsible for permanently changing farming practices in the regions of its influence around the world.

5. Explain why rural life has been consistently dominated by primary economic activities regardless of place or time period.

Chapter 8

Advanced Placement Topic VI

Industrialization and Economic Development

Note: Questions on this topic will comprise thirteen to seventeen percent of the Advanced Placement examination.

A. The Topic in Context - An Introduction

In a world becoming more globalized, human geographers are challenged to understand and interpret economies of scale. These identify the various levels of development across the world's regions. In some areas, people live at the subsistence level as marginalized farmers on meager patches of unproductive land, but in others, they cultivate thousands of acres on commercial farms using the latest technology and applying the principles of agribusiness. In yet other places, some people prosper in cities providing services through one the professions or in managerial positions for multi-national and transnational corporations. In the same urban setting, others endure low-paying jobs requiring minimal literacy or only the most basic of skills.

Enormous gaps exist between rich and poor classes within many countries and between rich and poor countries as well. Regional disparities abound. In some places the pace of economic change is so rapid it is staggering. Growth is constant and powerful. In other areas, economies stagnate with millions of workers idle or only seasonally employed. Families barely exist on the fringe of survival. Life changes little. People live in abject poverty eking out minimal livings for themselves and their children often in subhuman conditions.

Economic geographers use a variety of strategies to explain why these disparities exist, why they are so extreme, why they are where they are, and how they can be eliminated - or at least narrowed. One recent approach is to analyze regional and national economies using the core-periphery model as a means of understanding the economic relationships among places. This model views the world as an integrated whole where the laws of change are anything but absolute. It recognizes that development is complex and cannot be reduced to simple categories. A variety of factors, then, determines growth or decline at both the core and the periphery.

The economic stability of the contemporary world is being shaped by industrialization. Indeed in many places, it is the only key to development, with the possible exception of tourism. Even agriculture has been either diminished as a primary activity or even totally abandoned.

For prosperity to result from industrializing, care must be given to the location of plants and factories so that they have all the elements of production assuring economic success in an increasingly specialized world (i.e., a single item's parts being made in many places and sent to a single location for assembly and transport to other places across the globe). As a result, the manufacture of goods in recent decades means that industry is presently undergoing a global shift with significant implications for the future in both the core and the periphery nations. The one factory town model, for example, that once characterized the economy of much of New England is now a relic.

Yet once industrialization has been realized, there is a another phase of economic development. It is the transition that shifts an economy from production to service and ultimately from service to the processing and analysis of information. Human geographers call these phenomena deindustrialization. What this means is that declining industrialization in the core is fundamentally altering global patterns of economic well-being largely because labor-intensive manufacturing has moved to the periphery.

The entire realm of economic geography is in transition. It is in search of new definitions and new models. The role of world cities is a case in point. These are the control centers that host the multinational and supranational cores that drive the global economy. Their role and function transcends national boundaries. What occurs in one part of the world may well be the result of a decision made in a city half a world away. In many ways, these cities are increasingly doing for finance, production, and distribution what has typically been the role of nation-states. What is emerging, then, is a new world economic order far more complex and far more difficult to understand than the former and more simple systems.

B. Focus Question to Direct Topic VI Inquiry

When students have concluded their study of this topic, they should be able to prepare a comprehensive answer to this question:

What are the forces of modern economic change that encourage some national economies to grow and flourish and others to either stagnate or decline?

C. Key Words/Definitions

Students should be able to define these terms and use each in such a way that its meaning is clear in the context of a sentence. Example:

Definition - Cartel: a combination of independent business organizations formed to regulate production, pricing, and marketing of goods by the members

Context Sentence - The Organization of Petroleum Exporting Countries (OPEC) is a cartel in which joint pricing policies are largely responsible for the cost of gas at the pump in the United States.

Note: The citations within the parentheses next to each term identify where it is defined and/or discussed in *Human Geography: Culture, Society, and, Space* (Seventh Edition). Many terms are also included in the Glossary in Resource C

agglomeration (350, 371)
basic/non-basic activities (Reference section)
break-of-bulk point (381)
cartel (373)
core region (339)
core-periphery model (398-399)
dependency theory (401)
developed country (396)
developing country (398)
economic reach (343)

economic tiger (Reference section)
economic sector (272-273)
entrepôt (Reference section)
feudalism (228)
globalization (263, 409)
Gross National Product (GNP) (396-398)
industrial location theory (371-375)
infrastructure (374-375)
least cost theory (371)
liberal models (399)
manufacturing export zones (421)
maquiladora (393)
mercantilism (Reference section)
Modernization Model of Economic Development (Reference section)
Multinational unions (244)
multiplier effect (343)
natural resource (Reference section)
new international division of labor (414-416)
North American Free Trade Agreement (NAFTA) (247, 393)
per capita (Reference section)
peripheral region (399)
postindustrial (Reference section)
primary economic activity (Reference section)
primary industrial region (379)
renewable resource (Reference section)
secondary economic activity (373)
secondary industrial region (392-394)
semi-peripheral region (399)
Special Economic Zones (SEZs) (392)
structuralist model (399)
tertiary economic activity (273)
time-space compression (424)
underdevelopment (396, 398)
variable cost (370)
Weber's least cost theory (371)
world city model (418-420)
world systems theory "Industrial Location Theory," (223, 399)

D. Detailed Topic Outline/Text Correlation

Note: The citations within the parentheses identify where information within the outline can be located in *Human Geography: Culture, Society, and Space* (Seventh Edition).

VI. Topic - Industrialization and Economic Development

A. Character of industrialization (Note: Students will find that "A Changing World" (403-405) provides a brief but comprehensive introduction to Topic VI by showing the relationship between politics and economics in a world community becoming increasingly more globalized.)
    1. Economic sectors: primary, secondary, tertiary, and quaternary (272-273)
    2. Specialization in places and the concept of comparative advantage (380)

3. Transport and communications (398, 373-374)
4. Models of industrial location (Figure 26-1 on 369-376, 400-401)

B. Spatial aspects of the rise of industrial economies
    1. Changing energy sources and technology (375, 547-549, 460)
    2. Economic cores and peripheries (398-399)
    3. Models of economic development and their geographic critiques (396-398, 399-400)

C. Contemporary global patterns of industrialization/resource extraction (Note: Chapter 25)
    1. Linkages and interdependencies (373)
    2. Changing patterns of industrial activity and deindustrialization (42-423)

D. Impacts of industrialization (Note: Chapter 33 deals with the topics in this section extensively. It examines how humans have altered the environment over the millennia and how in recent years, they have been able to affect environmental change on a global scale both positively and negatively.)
    1. Time-space compression ("Industrial Location Theory," 371-375)
    2. Social stratification (cf. "structuralist theory" on 399)
    3. Health, quality of life, and hazards ("Nonvectored Infectious Diseases" and "Chronic Diseases," 472-476)
    4. Environmental change and issues of sustainability (541-554)

E. Topic VI Study Questions - Industrialization and Economic Development

1. Define economic geography.
2. Compare and contrast the differences that distinguish the developing from the developed world
3. Describe some of the disparities in the core-periphery relationships among different regions of the world.
4. Discuss the relationship between politics and economic development. Use specific examples to illustrate the points you make in your essay.
5. Select one of the two models for development (i.e., liberal or structuralist) described in the chapter and analyze its strengths and weaknesses in terms of facilitating or inhibiting a country's economic growth.
6. Describe the five stages of Rostow's "modernization model." Evaluate its accuracy as a predictor of a country's struggle for economic development.
7. Describe location theory. Discuss how it helps explain the spatial positioning of industries and their success or failure.
8. Explain why there are regional economic differences within a country.
9. Describe Weber's least cost theory. Explain why it has been so hotly debated among economic geographers.
10. Describe the physical and human features commonly shared by the world's four major industrial regions (i.e., Western and Central Europe, Eastern North America, Russia-Ukraine, Eastern Asia).
11. Using a cultural and an environmental perspective, evaluate the major positive and negative impacts of industrialization.
12. Explain the causes of deindustrialization. Explain why the tertiary and quatenary economic sectors are the replacements for industrialization.
13. Evaluate the importance of the maquiladora as new economic expressions in the world economy.

F. Researching Topic VI - Industrialization and Economic Development

Students will find that preparing short research papers (i.e., up to five pages) as part of the study of a topic is an effective means of deepening their understanding of its meaning and purpose within the realm of human geography. Such research serves not only as an introduction to the resources available about the topic but also as a strategy for applying the skills of organization and presentation essential to responding to the extended answer questions on the Advanced Placement examination in Human Geography.

The topics provided here are certainly not comprehensive and all-inclusive, but only serve as suggestions for the kind of research and investigation students can undertake. Each research paper should be written from an outline developed from the student's research with a brief introduction stating the hypothesis (i.e., a tentative explanation that accounts for a set of facts that will be tested by the investigation presented in the paper). A hypothesis, then, is merely a theory or a speculation that the researcher sets out to prove or disprove.

The body of the research paper provides the detail addressing the hypothesis. It provides precise information derived from the research the student has done and also follows the outline that has been prepared. As a result, the arguments should be well organized and logically presented. Including anecdotes and examples will make the paper more convincing and also more persuasive.

The final part of the research paper is the conclusion. That is the section providing a summary of what the student has argued and joins those arguments to the hypothesis. The purpose of the conclusion is to demonstrate why the hypothesis works (or does not work). It is the part of the paper where the writer rests the case.

To be convincing, research papers should contain citations and bibliographies. That gives them credibility and it also helps validate the arguments the student presents. Because there is no *one* correct way to document research these days, teachers will provide the necessary guidance and direction for students There are several widely used style manuals available. However, the three most often used to guide reporting research in human geography include:

American Psychological Association. *Publication Manual of the American Psychological Association*. 4th ed. Washington, D. C.: American Psychological Association. 1994.

Gibaldi, Joseph *MLA Handbook for Writers of Research Papers*. 4th ed. New York: Modern Language Association. 1995.

The Chicago Manual of Style. 14th ed. Chicago: University of Chicago Press. 1993.

Some Suggested Research Topics on Industrialization and Economic Development

Defining the Developed and the Developing World
The Gross National Product and the Quality of Life in the Developing World: Exploring A Relationship
Examining A Pre-Industrial Society: A Case Study (e.g., Niger, Mali, Burkina Faso, Somalia, etc.)
Why Some Countries Are Rich and Some Countries Are Poor: An Analysis
Alfred Weber and His Theories of Industrial Location: An Explanation

Geopolitics: An Authentic Inquiry Model or a Pseudo Science?
Tourism as an Economic Activity
Politics and Economic Development: An Essential Relationship
What Makes A Corporation Transnational?
New Economic Expressions: Distinguishing Between Quarternary and Quinary Industries
The International Division of Labor: Measuring Its Value

G. Connecting to *Human Geography in Action*

Chapter 6 (6-1 to 6-22) provides some practical applications of economic geography. In addition to reinforcing information about the several levels of economic activity described in *Human Geography: Culture, Society, and Space* (Seventh Edition), it asks students to compare their state's economic profile to the national profile now and thirty years earlier. It also provides some exercises that relate to the contemporary job market showing the relationship between geography (location, site, access to transport and materials, etc.) and jobs using regional multipliers.

H. Sample Multiple-Choice Questions

These questions are typical of the kinds of questions students can expect on the examination in Advanced Placement Human Geography. Reviewing the section on multiple-choice questions in Chapter 1 will help students better orient themselves for selecting the appropriate answer in the sample questions included here.

Directions: Each of the questions or incomplete statements is followed by five suggested answers or completions. Select the one that is best in each case.

1. Which of these factors is vital to economic development?
    A. a population with a high doubling time
    B. a country with a high Gross National Product
    C. an available and abundant natural resource
    D. a well developed transport system
    E. a high literacy rate

2. What term do economic geographers use to identify organizations promoting political, economic, and/or cultural cooperation to promote some shared objective?
    A. supranational
    B. international
    C. traditional
    D. interdependent
    E. national

3. What is the main focus of activities functioning in the tertiary sector of an economic system?
    A. automobile manufacturing
    B. agriculture
    C. acquiring and processing information
    D. hunting and fishing
    E. providing services

4. What is the function of the maquiladora in the modern-day economy?
    A. These are foreign-owned plants that assemble imported goods for export.

B. These are factory incentive zones that have been funded in the cities of the developing world by the International Monetary Fund.

C. These are a category of agricultural migrant workers who receive government subsidies to settle permanently in Latin America's industrial cities.

D. These are cattle ranches in the Rio Grande Valley that grow cattle for export to the protein-deprived countries in the developing world.

E. These are high energy consumption regions in eastern North America and Western Europe where nuclear power is the primary energy source.

5. What two features best characterize the changes affected by the Industrial Revolution?
   A. service industries and information processing
   B. technological innovation and specialization
   C. improved farm implements and the development of hybrid seeds
   D. higher literacy rates and decreased population doubling time
   E. well-equipped professional armies and the deployment of nuclear weapons

6. What element is basic to Weber's least cost theory in determining the location of an industrial site?
   A. power supplies
   B. labor costs
   C. availability of transportation
   D. proximity to markets
   E. quantity of raw materials

7. Which of these statements about core-periphery relationships is correct in characterizing the global economic system?
   A. It works to the advantage of periphery countries.
   B. It works to the disadvantage of core countries.
   C. It works to the advantage of both core and periphery countries.
   D. It works to the disadvantage of periphery countries.
   E. It is irrelevant in a complex worldwide economic system.

8. In Walt Rostow's modernization model identifying the levels and stages of economic development, in what sector of the economy are most workers employed in those few countries achieving the fifth stage?
   A. extractive
   B. service
   C. industrial
   D. professional
   E. agricultural

9. All of the following are typical criteria for determining if a country is developing and peripheral except
   A. a high birth rate.
   B. a high infant mortality rate.
   C. a high unemployment rate.
   D. a high energy consumption per capita rate.
   E. a high per capita GNP rate

10. The growth or decline of secondary industries can be influenced by factors not always accounted for by models but determined by such factors as
    A. political instability.
    B. the availability of raw materials.
    C. an adequate labor force.
    D. access to transportation.
    E. a reasonable agglomeration.

Answers: 1) E 2) A 3) E 4) A 5) B 6) C 7) D 8) B 9) D 10) A

I. Sample Free-Response Questions

These questions are similar to the free-response items likely to be on the Advanced Placement Human Geography examination.

1. Explain why there are regional economic differences within a country.

2. Select one of the development models that human geographers use to assess a country's economic progress. Evaluate its strengths and weaknesses.

3. Analyze Weber's least cost theory as it relates to the processes of Japan's industrialization resulting from the Meiji Restoration in 1867.

4. Compare the challenges of economic development in any two of the world's developing countries.

5. Provide three reasons why tourism is a mixed blessing for peripheral nations. Discuss each one as it positively and negatively affects local economies.

Chapter 9

Advanced Placement Topic VII

Cities and Urban Land Use

Note: Questions on this topic will comprise thirteen to seventeen percent of the Advanced Placement examination. Part Seven of the text most closely correlates to the information needed for AP Topic Seven.

A. The Topic in Context - An Introduction

After the invention of agriculture, more densely populated settlements were its logical extension. With farms able to provide a constant and generally reliable food supply for large numbers of people, it was possible for human groups to cluster in places varying in size, composition, location, arrangement and function, and address issues beyond the basic struggle to acquire the essentials of food, clothing, and shelter. Known variously over the centuries as hamlets, villages, towns, and cities, these groupings of habitation have become the focus of most aspects of life. They are centers of social and economic activities, political and administrative systems, transportation and communication networks, and cultural and educational opportunities. As such, they exercise a powerful influence on styles of life, on the development of patterns of culture, and on the quality of contacts groups have with each other. Although settlements across the world differ markedly, nonetheless knowing their processes and functions is central to a knowledge of human geography.

Cities as the largest and densest of human settlements have become the nodes of modern society. Now almost half of the world's people live in them. Indeed in some of its industrialized regions, seventy-five percent of the population inhabits urban areas. The trend of rapid growth is a constant everywhere. Such cities as Tokyo, Cairo, and São Paulo cover vast areas where population densities number in the hundreds - even thousands - per square mile. And the phenomenon of megalopolis, a web of interconnected metropolitan areas such as the one stretching from Washington, D.C. to Boston, is an undeniable reality everywhere in the world.

But not all urban growth has been as intense as it is today. Historically, cities have evolved in stages. The fortress city of the ancient world became the administrative and trading center of later times. With the Industrial Revolution, factory-dominated manufacturing cores replaced the earlier city models that were the focus of commerce, learning, and religion. With the coming of the automobile, these factory towns gave way to the suburbanized modern cities where great tracts of land have been transformed from rural to urban uses at increasingly greater distances from the old downtowns. And now human geographers are beginning to study the emergence of the postmodern city, a product of technologically advanced societies. As an entrepreneurial and information center, its function is clear, but its form is not.

The urbanization that has become one of the connecting threads of the modern world is not problem-free. Urban influences have significantly affected human geography. Primate cities, megacities, and megalopolises exercise preeminent influences on the culture, politics, economics, and social values of their countries. Wherever their location, their problems are cross-cultural. Such problems may differ in degree but not in kind. Pollution, strained infrastructures, substandard housing, congestion, crime, and poor schools are as evident in the cities of North and South America as they are in Europe, Asia, or Africa. These conditions stand in sharp contrast to the vitality and energy also associated with modern cities. Learning to reduce these contrasts and improve the quality of urban life is the challenge all cities face.

B. Focus Question to Direct Topic VII Inquiry

When students have concluded their study of this topic, they should be able to prepare a comprehensive answer to this question:

Compare and contrast the similarities and differences among the cities of the ancient world, those of preindustrial Europe, and modern cities designed on western models.

C. Key Words/Definitions

Students should be able to define these terms and use each in such a way that its meaning is clear in the context of a sentence. Example:

Definition - <u>Urban System</u>: the functional and spatial organization of cities (e.g., transportation modes, street design and layout, the location of shopping and recreation areas, etc.)

Context Sentence - As Brasilia was being conceptualized as Brazil's capital city, planners had the opportunity to invent an entirely new <u>urban system</u>.

Note: The citations within the parentheses next to each term identify where it is defined and/or discussed in *Human Geography: Culture, Society, and Space* (Seventh Edition). Many terms are also included in the Glossary in Resource C

agglomeration (350, 371)
Borchert, John (335)
central business district (CBD) (335, 337)
central place (343-344)
central place theory (344-346)
Christaller, Walter (344-346)
concentric zone model (336)
deglomeration (433)
feudal city (324)
gentrification (359, 434)
hamlet (294, 330)
hinterland (329-30)
Industrial Revolution (76, 282, 300, 349, 369, 370)
infrastructure (374-375)
inner city (433)
megacity (332, 351, 356-357)
megalopolis (331, 355)
mercantile city (326)
metropolis (331)
multiple nuclei model (336-337)
postmodern city (Reference section)
preindustrial city (223, 325)
primate city (324, 327)
sector model (336)

site (333)
situation (331)
social stratification (40)
suburb (330-331, 336, 338)
urban form (330)
urban function (330, 342)
urban geography (329)
urban hierarchy (330, 346)
urban models (344)
urban morphology (Reference section)
urban realms (337)
urban site (333)
urban system (321)
urbanization (313-363)
village (294-296, 330)
world city (418-420)
zoning (357)

D. Detailed Topic Outline/Text Correlation

Note: The citations within the parentheses identify where information within the outline can be located in *Human Geography: Culture, Society, and Space* (Seventh edition).

VII. Topic - Cities and Urban Land Use

A. Definitions of Urbanism (316-317)

B. Origin and evolution of cities (Chapter 21 on "Urbanization and Civilization" offers a complete discussion of this topic, 315-327)
      1. Historical patterns of urbanization (Chapter 21 provides comprehensive coverage showing the evolution of cities from ancient times to the present, 315-327.)
      2. Cultural context and urban form (Comments on agglomeration, specialization, urban geography and the ranking of urban centers are especially helpful, 329-331.)
      3. Urban growth and rural-urban migration (John Borchert's model provides an historical context on this sub-topic, 335)
      4. Rise of megacities (456-357)
      4. Models of urban systems (335-339.
      5. Comparative models of internal city structure (The essay on "Models of UrbanStructure" in Chapter 22, 335-339, describes the differences in the form of cities in various parts of the world. Chapter 23 on "Changing Cities in a Changing World" also examines the structure of cities around the world and discusses the impact of globalization on them as well as the emergence of world cities in the late twentieth century, 348-362.)

C. Functional character of contemporary cities (Chapter 23, 348-362)
      1. Changing employment mix (342-344)
      2. Changing demographic and social structures
D. Built environment and social space
      1. Transportation and infrastructure (373-375)

2. Political organization of urban areas (While this sub-topic is not directly addressed in the text, the broad frameworks of urban politics are covered in Chapter 25, "Political Culture and the Evolving State," 201-218. Students will find it beneficial to review this section of the text. The introduction and the section on "Political Culture" will be particularly timely as well, 202-203.)
3. Patterns of race, ethnicity, gender, and class (Chapters 31 and 32 provide a comprehensive treatment of these issues)

E. Responses to urban growth
    1. Urban planning and design
    2. Community action and initiatives (This is an open-ended topic not typically covered in human geography textbooks. It can be best explored through case studies on selected local issues - e.g., community policing, urban block clubs, neighborhood action groups, local school councils, etc. as well as through research investigations of similar issues affecting cities beyond the United States.)

* Because "Edge City" is a relatively recent term in the vocabulary of urban geography, it is not yet discussed in most urban geography textbooks. Edge cities are largely an American phenomena of the late twentieth century and identify satellites of such old and established cities as Boston, Chicago, New York, San Francisco, etc. These new urban inventions are characterized by corporate parks, shopping malls, complexes of motels and hotels, convention centers, entertainment cores, and subdivisions of single family homes. Originally rural village centers set up to service local truck farmers, these curious new urban cores now ring the great cities through freeway connections and easy access routes to a major regional or international airport.

For a full treatment of the topic, refer to: Joel Garreau, <u>Edge City: Life on the New Frontier</u>. New York: Doubleday. 1991.

E. Topic VII Study Questions - Cities and Urban Land Use

1. Describe the difference between site and situation as each relates to urban location
2. Discuss the role of the "world city." Why is it a twentieth century phenomenon?
3. Identify the varieties of design in ancient cities. Explain the reasons for the variations.
4. What are the characteristics of the primate city?
5. What are the differences among mercantile cities, manufacturing cities, and modern cities?
6. Explain the relationship between social stratification and urban elites.
7. Why are urban places ranked?
8. What are hinterlands? Explain the role they play in the organization of urban places.
9. Give several reasons explaining why megalopolises exist the modern world.
10. Distinguish between a megacity and a megalopolis.
11. Analyze the significance of Christaller's central place theory.
12. What made urban planning attractive to many city officials and civic groups in the United States in the early twentieth century?
13. Explain how cities in Africa, Latin America and Asia differ from those in North America and Europe.
14. Analyze the positive and negative impacts of urban gentrification.
15. What factors explain both agglomeration and deglomeration in the rise and decline of cities?

F. Researching Topic VII - Cities and Urban Land Use

Students will find that preparing short research papers (i.e., up to five pages) as part of the study of a topic is an effective means of deepening their understanding of its meaning and purpose within the realm of human geography. Such research serves not only as an introduction to the resources available about the topic but also as a strategy for applying the skills of organization and presentation essential to responding to the extended answer questions on the Advanced Placement examination in Human Geography.

The topics provided here are certainly not comprehensive and all-inclusive, but only serve as suggestions for the kind of research and investigation students can undertake. Each research paper should be written from an outline developed from the student's research with a brief introduction stating the hypothesis (i.e., a tentative explanation that accounts for a set of facts that will be tested by the investigation presented in the paper). A hypothesis, then, is merely a theory or a speculation that the researcher sets out to prove or disprove.

The body of the research paper provides the detail addressing the hypothesis. It provides precise information derived from the research the student has done and also follows the outline that has been prepared. As a result, the arguments should be well organized and logically presented. Including anecdotes and examples will make the paper more convincing and also more persuasive.

The final part of the research paper is the conclusion. That is the section providing a summary of what the student has argued and joins those arguments to the hypothesis. The purpose of the conclusion is to demonstrate why the hypothesis works (or does not work). It is the part of the paper where the writer rests the case.

To be convincing, research papers should contain citations and bibliographies. That gives them credibility and it also helps validate the arguments the student presents. Because there is no *one* correct way to document research these days, teachers will provide the necessary guidance and direction for students. There are several widely used style manuals available. However, the three most often used to guide reporting research in human geography include:

American Psychological Association. *Publication Manual of the American Psychological Association*. 4th ed. Washington, D. C.: American Psychological Association. 1994.

Gibaldi, Joseph *MLA Handbook for Writers of Research Papers*. 4th ed. New York: Modern Language Association. 1995.

The Chicago Manual of Style. 14th ed. Chicago: University of Chicago Press. 1993.

Some Suggested Research Topics for Cities and Urban Land Use

A Non-Western Urban Model: A Case Study
Cities as Economic Entities
Hexagons and Honeycombs: Christaller's "Central Places"
Models of Urban Development: A Critical Analysis
Patterns of Urban Hierarchies: Studies in Diffusion
Racial Segregation in American Cities: An Historical Overview
Suburban Development in the United States
The Postmodern City: Some Predictions and Speculations

Ancient and Modern Athens: A Comparative Analysis
Urban Planning and the "Ideal City"
Why the Megalopolis?

G. Connecting to *Human Geography in Action*

Chapter 9 (9-1 to 9-22 plus CD) introduces students to both central place theory and the structure of urban hierarchies by providing both clear explanations and practical application activities. Students will learn about the threshold of a function by examining the relationship between the size of a city and the number of pizza parlors it is able to support (9--9 to 9-13) and the difference between low-order and high-order central place functions by evaluating maps showing the distribution of major and minor league baseball teams. The maps in this exercise are generated by a Geographic Information System (GIS).

In Chapter 10 (10-1 to 10-16), students develop single-page profiles of census tracts based on statistics gathered from government documents. The activity also provides opportunities to learn about "edge cities" and how they function. Figure 10.3 (10-5) uses metropolitan Philadelphia as a case in point to illustrate this emerging phenomenon.

H. Sample Multiple-Choice Questions

These questions are typical of the kinds of questions students can expect on the examination in Advanced Placement Human Geography. Reviewing the section on multiple-choice questions in Chapter 1 will help students better orient themselves for selecting the appropriate answer in the sample questions included here.

Directions: Each of the questions or incomplete statements is followed by five suggested answers or completions.. Select the one that is best in each case.

1. Which of the following has most affected the development of suburbs in the United States in the last 50 years?
        A. popularity of the automobile
        B. inexpensive and reliable electrical energy
        C. computer technology and the internet
        D. high-speed rail transportation
        E. access to regional airports

2. What statement best characterizes a feature of the concentric zone model of urban development?
        A. A multi-metropolitan complex is formed by the coalescence of two or more major urban areas.
        B. Urban growth conforms to sectors radiating out from the downtown along such transportation routes as bus and train lines.
        C. The city is organized into groupings of specialized activities (e.g., housing districts, shopping areas, port facilities, etc.).
        D. The central business district (CBD) is the focus of the city's social, commercial, and civic life.
        E. City growth is haphazard following no particular design or predictable formula of development.

3. Which of the following economic activities is most likely to be found in a city's central business district (CBD)?
    A. an automobile dealership
    B. a transfer point for railroad freight cars
    C. an office tower
    D. a metal fabricating plant
    E. the production facility of a major textbook publisher

Note: Use the following essay to answer questions 4 through 7.

Urban Growth in the Netherlands

The Netherlands is one of the most densely populated countries in Europe. Most of the people live in its highly urbanized western part - an area known as the Randstad. The Randstad includes two dense population clusters. In the north are the cities of Haarlem, Amsterdam, Hilversum, and Utrecht; in the south there are Leyden, The Hague, Rotterdam, and Dordrecht. Between these two urban groupings is a line of continuous settlement but that area is less densely populated. It is called the Green Heart.

Over the years, the urban growth of the Randstad has been significant. Less than a hundred years ago, its cities were quite small and set far apart from one another. By 1900, as a result of the impact of the Industrial Revolution, the population of the cities rapidly increased. As the economy of the Netherlands developed, tens of thousands of job opportunities became available, and people poured into the growing urban clusters from the country's rural areas.

Within fifty years, the Randstad had become a huge urban complex. The growth was expected to continue for many more years, but by 1960, the number of people living in the four largest cities had begun to decline. Growth was spilling over into the suburban areas of the Green Heart. People left for a number of reasons. Many of the older homes had become hazardous and uncomfortable. The need for space for new office buildings, hotels, and assembly facilities meant that old structures were torn down. This decreased the housing supply. Thus people were attracted to the greenery of the suburbs away from the noise and traffic that had become a part of urban life.

4. What is the term urban geographers use to identify the settlement patterns that have developed since industrialization in the Randstad and the population growth in the Green Heart?
    A. urban core
    B. metropolis
    C. protruded areas
    D. central business district
    E. megalopolis

5. What accounted for the growth of the Randstad after 1900?
    A. increasing job opportunities in the cities
    B. decline in agricultural production
    C. dam and dike programs to control flooding
    D. rapid development of affordable housing in urban areas
    E. improved transport systems connecting the Randstad with the Green Heart

6. Why did many people leave the urban centers of the Randstad in the 1960s?

A. The economy weakened resulting in massive layoffs.
B. The Dutch government intervened to control the growth of cities.
C. The demand for commercial space caused a housing shortage.
D. Transportation networks made outlying areas more accessible.
E. The Dutch economy became more dispersed due to changing patterns of trade.

7. Human geographers identify the attractive features of the Green Heart that encouraged migration away from the core cities of the Randstad as
   A. push factors.
   B. pull factors.
   C. gentrification.
   D. threshold of function.
   E. travel effort.

8. On what principle is the hierarchy of urban places primarily based?
   A. population and their function and services
   B. their site and situation
   C. the availability of customized services
   D. the dominance of a single downtown serving as the urban core
   E. the number of basic industries providing job opportunities

9. Compare Figure 18-7 (248) to Figure 24.3 (330) to identify the statement identifying the most appropriate relationship established by the data on the two maps.
   A. The data presented is so inconsistent and contradictory that no valid relationship can be drawn.
   B. There is a high correlation between cities that have populations beyond 15 million and those serving major global financial roles.
   C. World cities and those with large populations tend to cluster in the southern hemisphere.
   D. Population size has little impact on the financial role a city plays in the world economy.
   E. Africa and most of Asia and the Pacific Rim play no role in the world economy.

10. All of the following account for the success of modern urban centers except
   A. their external locational attributes.
   B. their relative location with reference to non-local places.
   C. the physical qualities of the areas they occupy.
   D. their distance from other urban centers.
   E. their relatively easy access to other places.

Answers: 1) A 2) D 3) C 4) E 5) A 6) C 7) B 8) A 9) B 10) C

I. Sample Free-Response Questions

These questions are similar to the free-response items likely to be on the Advanced Placement Human Geography examination.

1. Describe a hinterland and explain why it is important in determining the hierarchies of urban places.

2. Evaluate the positive and negative factors that influence a city's site and situation. Provide examples to illustrate the points you make.

3. Compare the preindustrial city with the emerging model of the postmodern city.

4. Describe the characteristics of a primate city.

5. Explain why role and function are determining factors in a city's success.

Chapter 10

The Vocabulary of Advanced Placement Revisited: Prepping to be a Successful Test Taker Including Multiple Choice Sample Test

Multiple Choice Questions

Typically there are 80 questions in the multiple-choice section of the Advanced Placement history/social science examinations (including human geography). The difficulty is intentionally set at such a level that a candidate has to answer 50 to 60 percent of the questions correctly to receive a 3. Random guessing is discouraged, but students having some knowledge of the question and who can eliminate one or more choices and then select what they reason to be the best answer from the remaining choices, are likely to have some success. But the key to performing well on a multiple choice test is to read each question carefully in order to understand its purpose and connect it to what has been learned in the study of human geography.

Questions are distributed among the topics that define the course of studies in human geography as well as the concepts fundamental to understanding the principles of the discipline. Since geographers use models to replicate, explain, and predict reality, it is important to know what such models are and the theories that serve as the hypotheses on which they are based.

The questions included here are examples of the kinds that may typically appear on Advanced Placement exams. They represent categories that range from being able to recognize specific data in some detail to more sophisticated analytical questions, including those challenging students to differentiate among conflicting causes and their effects. The most challenging questions are those that call for interpretation and evaluation.

Recall: These are fact-based questions that require students to recollect specific information.

1. A unique form of rural settlement developed in French Canada is known as
   - A. long lots.
   - B. village centered agriculture.
   - C. riverside communes.
   - D. township and range segments.
   - E. extended homesteads.

2. People who practice slash and burn agriculture make their living as
   - A. subsistence farmers.
   - B. nomadic herders.
   - C. hunters and gatherers.
   - D. guest workers.
   - E. stateless migrants.

Determining Cause: The word "because" is always a part of the stem in this category of question. The student is expected to identify a reason for something.

3. The Brazilian economy prospered in the 1960s and early 1970s but in the decade that followed, it suffered a significant collapse because
   - A. there was a fall in the price of coffee.
   - B. the country amassed a staggering foreign debt.

C. the cost of imported fuel escalated.
D. the democratic government was overthrown.
E. development was concentrated in the Atlantic coastal cities.

4. The geographer Ellsworth Huntington believed that certain civilizations were more advanced than others because of
        A. irredentism.
        B. chance breakthroughs.
        C. the overall accessibility of certain world regions.
        D. climate factors.
        E. transculturation.

Interpreting Maps and Other Graphics: Students are provided a visual prompt that they must analyze and then identify the correct answer. Questions 5 and 6 require analysis and interpretation of a table, diagram, and map. Each is referenced to a graphic in *Human Geography: Culture, Society, and Space* (Seventh Edition) on the page identified in the body of the question.

5. Using Table 26-1 (Per Capita GNP) on 397, what reservation is an economic geographer likely to express about the economies of the countries listed after studying the data?
        A. The data do not reveal any of the details about national economies.
        B. Only the GNPs of very poor and very rich countries are provided.
        C. With the availability of more sophisticated data, GNP information is no longer a helpful tool in economic analysis.
        D. The table provides information too selective to be of any value in predicting a nation's economic strength.
        E. The table presents no information about the variations and inequities within the economies of the nations listed regardless of how strong or weak they are.

6. What is the purpose of Figure 22-10 on 345?
        A. to show the nesting of regions within regions in terms of their importance
        B. to show patterns of development on the rural landscape
        C. to indicate that only selected central places serve vital functions
        D. to illustrate how metropolitan areas are connected
        E. to provide information predicting a region's growth potential

Except Questions: AP multiple choice questions are never framed using negatives (i.e., Which of the following is <u>not</u> an example of cultural assimilation?). Rather the stem contains "except" as a way of having students discriminate among the possible responses.

7. All of the following have typically been true of plantation agriculture in Middle America except:
        A. It produces crops for export.
        B. It is an inefficient operation.
        C. It produces only a single crop.
        D. The capital and skills necessary to support it are imported.
        E. Labor on the plantations is seasonal.

8. All of these are rural economic activities presently operating in Eastern Colorado except
        A. cattle ranching.
        B. wheat farming.
        C. horse breeding.

Chapter 11

Advanced Placement Free-Response Sample Test: Suggestions and Strategies

All Advanced Placement courses are designed to prepare students for the examinations offered each May. That means learning for the test to earn the best possible score is central to the Advanced Placement experience. Effective test-taking is just as much a skill as using a textbook efficiently, or writing a comprehensive and well-organized research essay, or learning the vocabulary specific to a subject. Thus developing strategies to do well on the Advanced Placement Human Geography test is as important as knowing and understanding the content of the program of study itself.

Free-Response Questions

Students will have a prescribed amount of time to plan and write at least three essays in the free-response section of the Advanced Placement Human Geography exam. Therefore, it is essential that they not only manage their time well but also answer the questions asked as precisely and fully as possible. To do that, having a clear understanding of the meaning of the "operative" action verb will simplify the development of each essay. Being able to recall information is certainly important, but more important is understanding exactly what the question is asking. If, for example, a question indicates that you are to **evaluate** some aspect of human geography and you proceed only to **describe** it, then you have missed the point. Remember that an essay must directly answer the question asked. Thus student responses must be pointed and precise.

The seven verbs defined below represent key terms used on Advanced Placement exams. Sample question in human geography follow each definition. The notation in brackets refers to sections in *Human Geography: Culture, Society, and Space* (Seventh Edition) that provide information for preparing substantive answers.

Now that you have completed instruction, the best way to prep for the free-response questions is through practice. Utilizing the scenarios presented below, write a three-paragraph essay focusing on the operative verb specified. While you may wish to use your text as you complete these practice essays, better practice will come from using recall, as will be required on the actual examination.

1. **Analyze**: determine the component parts; examine the nature and relationship.

Using concepts from Part Eight of the text:
Analyze the spatial relationships between land values and prominent urban features (e.g., central business districts, open spaces near public parks, industrial sites, hotels and office development near an international airport). Incorporate information about Weber's industrial location theory as well as the von Thünen model. Include information about least cost theory.

2. **Assess/Evaluate**: judge the value or character of something; evaluate the positive and negative points; give an opinion regarding the value of something.

Using concepts from Part Seven of the text:
Evaluate the advantages and disadvantages of allowing foreign-owned businesses to purchase land, open factories or conduct other kinds of business in a host country. {Use information from

urban geography sections of the text. Also include information about globalization trends. Note, too, the relationship between trade and culture.

3. **Compare**: examine for the purposes of noting similarities and differences.

Using concepts from Part One and Two of the text:
Compare the geographic effects of migration streams and counter-streams of rural African Americans to northern urban centers earlier in the 20th century to those of the Irish who emigrated to the United States after the Potato Famine in 1848. {Note the difference between external migrations and internal migrations. Show the applications of expansion diffusion and relocation diffusion as they apply to both the African American and Irish experiences. Address the issue of the geography of dislocation when developing your answer.

4. **Contrast**: examine to show dissimilarities or points of difference.

Using concepts from Part Nine of the text:
Contrast the attitudes toward resource development and use by 19th century entrepreneurs and 20th century conservationists. Be sure to provide information relating to concepts and approaches as well as a reference to understanding environmental change.

5. **Describe**: give an account of; tell about; provide a word picture.

Using concepts from Parts Three, Four and Ten of the text:
Describe the relationship between the diffusion of language and religion. Be sure to note colonial influences and other cultural traits that may be impacted by the diffusion of language and religion.

6. **Discuss**: talk over; write about; consider or examine from various points of view; debate; present the various sides of the issue.

Using concepts from Part Five of the text:
Discuss the importance of the emerging supranational organizations (e.g., United Nations, European Union, Organization of African Unity, etc.) as political and economic expressions of new frameworks for dealing with such international issues as population policy, settling boundary disputes, and relocating refugees and other displaced people. Note especially information relating to regional multinational unions.

7. **Explain**: make clear; provide the causes or reasons for something; make known in detail; tell the meaning of.

Using concepts from Part Six of the text:
Explain the impact of the agricultural revolution on the human culture.

All seven content areas have been addressed in these practice free-response questions. For more information and additional practice free-response questions, go to the Advanced Placement course website at www.collegeboard.com/ap and refer to pages 26-27.

Chapter 12

Selected Readings: Anticipating Advanced Placement Human Geography

For many students, Advanced Placement Human Geography will be their first geography experience since elementary or middle school. For some, their likely recollection is a geography program organized around memorizing places on the map and matching capitals with states and countries, products with their places of origin, and major cities and regions with countries and continents. Although helpful in developing a mental map of Earth, such an exposure to geography is not very informative about the planet's physical and human systems and their interaction. Nor does it promote an awareness of the connections between and among places, or an understanding of the world in spatial terms. As valuable as the earlier school study might have been in promoting a core understanding of geography, the perspective was probably quite basic and narrow and not focused on promoting a view of the world that described the changing patterns of places or methods for unraveling their meaning.

Thus, this reading list. The books on it have been selected to help students understand the nature and complexity of geography before undertaking its formal study in the Advanced Placement Human Geography program. They will serve as an introduction to all the realms of geography but with a special emphasis on the elements of human geography. In its own way, each book will broaden students' knowledge of the discipline by helping make the complex simple, and the intricate interesting.

The list is quite eclectic. Each book offers an insight to what human geography is and how human geographers analyze and interpret the world. The books have been selected because they are easily accessible, eminently readable, broadly informative, and specifically focused on some important aspect of human geography such as urban development or religion and culture. Students who read from this list in anticipation of their Advanced Placement Human Geography course will not only enjoy the subject matter of the books they select but also develop a context that will make their Advanced Placement experience more meaningful.

Davis, Kenneth C. *Don't Know Much about Geography: Everything You Need to Know about the World but Never Learned* (New York: William Morrow and Company, Inc., 1992).
The author uses this book to popularize geography by making it a lively and fascinating inquiry on places, personalities, and events - but always in a spatial context. Written with humor and insight, Davis explains how geography plays a key role in shaping the destiny of nations and regions. He gives special emphasis to toponyms (i.e., the origin and meaning of place names) as a means of helping his readers understand Earth's complexity.

de Blij, H. J., *Harm de Blij's Geography Book: A Leading Geographer's Fresh Look at Our Changing World* (New York: John Wiley and Sons, Inc., 1995).
The author of the text for which the **Study Guide** has been prepared has provided a concise and focused overview of geography - what it is, how a knowledge of it is essential for understanding contemporary issues, and how it can be applied to inform the world view of Americans. Rich in interpretations of the physical and human phenomena of Earth, de Blij has included valuable insights (and anecdotes) on the role geography plays in illuminating today's political, economic, and social problems.

Demko, George J. with Agel, Jerome, and Boe, Eugene *Why in the World: Adventures in Geography* (New York: Doubleday/Anchor Books, 1992).

The authors entertainingly demonstrate that geography provides a multi-faceted look at the never-ending drama between the world's physical and cultural environments. It is an engaging introduction to the "new" geography that demonstrates how the physical and social sciences, and the humanities are joined through the lens of geography. The book also includes the biographies of 173 of the world's countries.

Garreau, Joel. *Edge City: Life on the New Frontier* (New York: Doubleday, 1991).
Garreau is a not a geographer, but in this exquisite monograph about new urban expressions, he shows the practical applications of geography to help his readers understand the way Americans have dramatically changed their cities in the late twentieth century. The book is a convincing study about the importance of the uses of human geography.

Hanson, Susan, ed. *Ten Geographic Ideas that Changed the World* (New Brunswick: Rutgers University Press, 1997).
In a series of thought-provoking and often witty essays, some of the most distinguished geographers in the United States explore and explain ten geographic ideas that have literally changed the world. They examine such topics as the power of maps in our lives as well as the importance of how and why we perceive places the way we do. The collection is an excellent introduction to modern geography.

Sherer, Thomas E., Jr. *The Complete Idiot's Guide™ to Geography* (New York: Alpha Books, 1997).
Even though the title of this book seems a bit impish, it provides solid information about the world and its regions, and how people and places interact. Through an extensive use of maps, the author helps the reader understand the why of where using trivia tidbits, anecdotes, and interesting descriptions of the history, culture and customs of each of the world's culture realms.

Tuan, Yi Fu *Passing Strange and Wonderful: Aesthetics, Nature and Culture* (Washington, D.C.: Island Press, 1993).
Beginning with the individual and the physical world, the author explores human progress from the simple to the complex. As a human geographer of great sensitivity and insight, Tuan subtly examines the moral and ethical aspects of the discipline. To guide his readers to a fuller understanding of human experience, he describes how the aesthetic operates in four widely disparate cultures: Australian aboriginal, Chinese, medieval European, and modern American.

Supplemental Resources

In addition to these introductions to human geography, there are other resources that will be valuable tools in the study of Advanced Placement Human Geography. This list identifies books that students can use to supplement *Human Geography: Culture, Society, and Space.* (Seventh Edition).

Espenshade, Edward B., Jr. ed. *Goode's World Atlas* (19th ed.) (Chicago: Rand McNally, 1995).
This is a comprehensive atlas that is well indexed for the easy location of thousands of the world's places. It is regionally organized but also contains sections of major city maps, thematic maps, and geographical tables.

Goodall. Brian *The Penguin Dictionary of Human Geography* (London: Penguin, 1987).
This book contains a glossary of terms necessary for a full understanding of the vocabulary special to the study of human geography.

Kapit, Wynn *The Geography Coloring Book* (New York: Harper Collins, 1991).
This unique, hands-on resource introduces students to the array of the world's regions by helping them visualize the location of places. Included for each of the maps to be colored is essential data (e.g., population, type of government, official language, predominant religions, etc.). The maps are simple in outline and detail and thus easy to use.

Webster's New Geographical Dictionary (Springfield, MA: Merriam-Webster, Inc. Publishers, 1988)
The thousands of entries in this reference volume provide basic information on the world's countries, regions, cities, and natural features. More than two hundred maps are also included.